"I have touched with a sense of art some people – they felt the love and the life. Can you offer me anything to compare to that joy for an artist?"

Mary Cassatt

# Cassatt

1844-1926

Author: Nathalia Brodskaïa
Translator: Sofya Hundt

Page 4
Photograph of Mary Cassatt

Layout
Baseline Co Ltd
127-129A Nguyen Hue
Fiditourist 3rd Floor
District 1, Ho Chi Minh City, Vietnam

ISBN 10: 1-84013-922-6
ISBN: 978-1-84013-922-8

Published in 2006 by Grange Books, an imprint of Grange Books Plc. The Grange Kingsnorth Industrial Estate Hoo, nr Rochester, Kent ME3 9ND www.grangebooks.co.uk



Printed in China

# Biography

1844: Birth of Mary Stevenson Cassatt near Pittsburgh in Pennsylvania. She is a daughter of a wealthy businessman. Before she is 10 years old, she visits numerous European capitals.

1851: She lives with her parents in Paris, and the following year she lives in Berlin.

1855: Her family goes back to the U.S.A

1860-65: Mary Cassatt studies at Pennsylvania Academy of Fine Arts despite her parents' objections.

1866: She goes back to Paris where she copies old masters in museums, especially in the Louvre. Jean-Léon Gérôme accepts her as a student.

1868: She visits Barbizon and is very eager to study its style. *Mandolin Player* is accepted by the Salon jury

1869: She is rejected by the Salon of Academic Art along with Cézanne, Monet and Sisley. Bazille, Degas, Pissarro and Renoir each have one work accepted.

1871-72: She lives with her mother in Rome, as do many American artists at this time, and travels throughout Europe: Italy, Spain, France etc.

1873-74: Creation of Salon des refusés. One of her paintings, *Offering the Panal to the Bullfighter*, is accepted by the Salon in Paris. She signs it "Mary Stevenson-Cassatt" using her middle name.

Mary Cassatt

1874: Anonymous Society of Painters, Sculptors, Printmakers, etc. exhibition, which is the first Impressionism show, takes place in Nadar's studio, 35 boulevard des Capucines. Cassatt, abroad, misses this event.

1877: Degas invites her to exhibit with the Impressionists. She also advises Louisine Havemeyer in buying Degas and other impressionists' paintings.

1878: Cassatt and Pissarro have a consistent correspondence indicating that they have a long friendship and professional collaboration. Cassatt admires Pissarro's work.

1879: Her work hangs in the Impressionism show. She begins a long friendship with Berthe Morisot and is very close to Degas. The latter asks Cassatt, Pissarro and Bracquemond to contribute to Le Jour et la Nuit. She remains an active Impressionism member until 1886 and buys several impressionist paintings especially for her brother, Alexander.

1882: Her sister Lydia dies.

1886: Her style evolves and she no longer identifies herself with any movement.

1890: She exhibits series of dry-points and aquatints and pastels in Durand-Ruel exhibition. She is strongly influenced by Japonese printmaking.

1890-1900: She is very active as an adviser to numerous art collectors.

1904: She receives the *Légion d'Honneur* for her contribution to the arts.

1926: She dies blind near Paris at the age of 82 years.

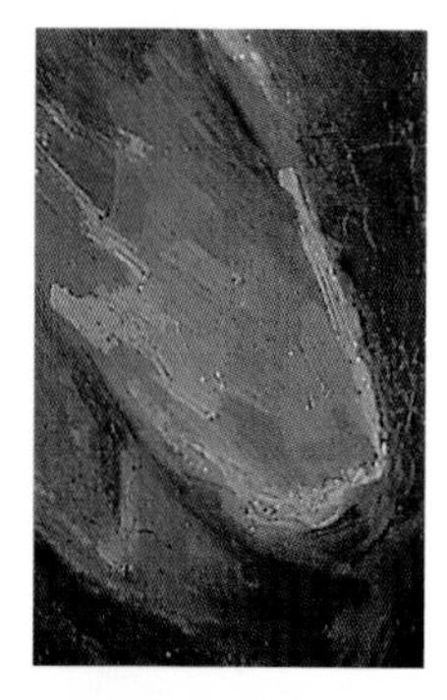

When she arrived in Paris in 1866, Mary Cassatt was twenty-two years old and she was one of many young Americans who had chosen to study in Paris. They arrived, painted in numerous Parisian academies and free studios, and met one another in the same "American" cafes, those little islands of homeland in foreign France where one spoke either English or terribly-accented French. After a while, they all returned home to become famous in their hometowns, or, at most, in their states. Mary, however, was the exception; she did not go back to America. Not only did she stay in France until the end of her life,

Bacchante

1872
Oil on canvas, 62 x 50.7 cm
Museum of American Art of the Pennsylvania
Academy of Fine Arts, Philadelphia, Pennsylvania

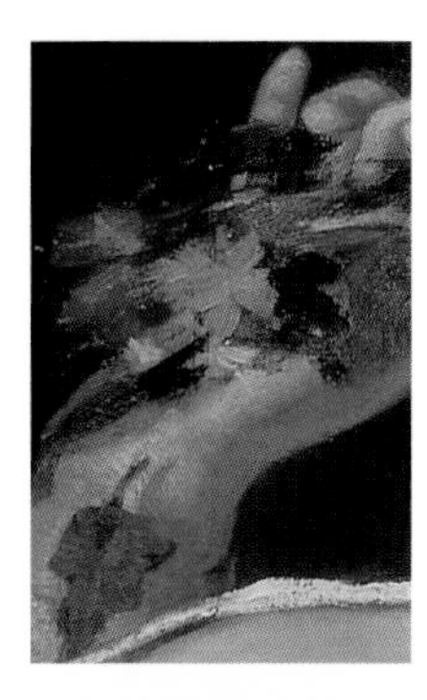

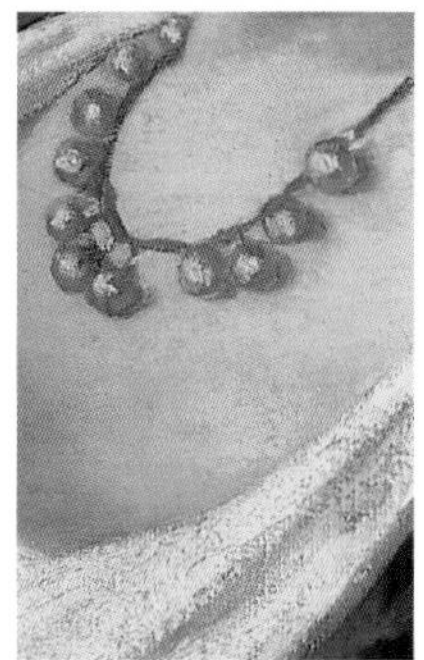

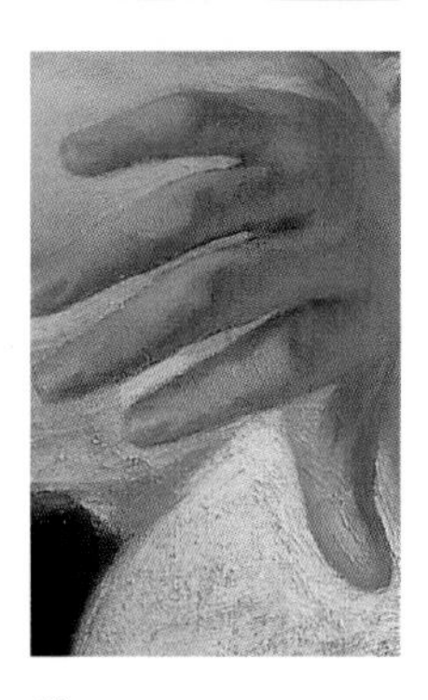

but she also devoted herself to Impressionism in defiance of the contemporary artistic conventions. Even among Impressionists, however, she was considered "strange," and she remained for them "a foreign impressionist". Mary never painted a single landscape, although it was precisely in landscape that the genre had originated, matured, and was expressed most vividly. Cassatt limited her work to only one intimate genre – depictions of women and children. Nevertheless, she was devoted to Impressionism such as she saw it in the work of Degas, her friend and mentor. She considered it an honour to exhibit her work together with that of Monet, Degas, Renoir, Sisley, Pissarro, and Berthe Morisot.

During Carnival

1872
Oil on canvas, 63.5 x 54.6 cm
Private Collection

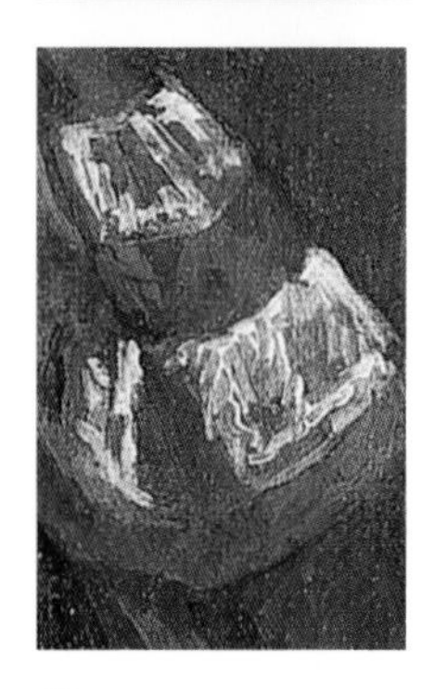

Mary fitted into this group quite naturally. She was not afraid of Paris's merciless, poisonous criticism, or the questionable privilege of being one of the rejects, even though before she joined the Impressionists her work had already been accepted by the Salon. She was incredibly gifted and unbelievably hardworking, and her French colleagues acknowledged this without fail. Mary Cassatt found her place among the best artists of her generation. She worked masterfully in oil and pastel, as well as the difficult and laborious graphic techniques. Her independence inspired respect. Only muchlater, however, at the end of the twentieth century,

Offering the Panal to the Bullfighter

1872-73
Oil on canvas, 100.6 x 85.1 cm
Sterling and Francine Clark Art Institute,
Williamstown, Massachusetts

was it recognised that Cassatt had accomplished the goal of future generations of artists. In fact, she had become the first artist of the School of Paris, which was formed at the beginning of the twentieth century. When young artists from Russia, Italy, Poland, Spain and Mexico began flocking to Paris, when Russian and American collectors became the first to purchase the new, shocking works of art, and when the literature of future American writers of renown was being born in the cafés of Montmartre and Montparnasse, the life of the blind artist Mary Cassatt was coming to an end at Château de Beaufresne in Mesnil-Théribus (Oise).

On a Balcony

1873

Oil on canvas, 101 x 54.6 cm

Philadelphia Museum of Art, Philadelphia, Pennsylvania

The enigma of Mary Cassatt began at her very birth. Some biographers regard 1845 as the year of her birth, and her tombstone in Le Mesnil-Théribus indicates May 24th 1845. However, it is probably best to trust family archives and parish records, which record her birthday as May 22nd 1844. She was born in the United States, in Allegheny, near Pittsburgh, Pennsylvania. As she proudly told her biographer at the end of her life: "I am an American," she said, "downright American... My mother is also an American, a daughter of Americans. Her family was of Scottish origin, who emigrated to America around 1700.

Spanish Dancer Wearing a Lace Mantilla

1873
Oil on canvas, 65 x 49.5 cm
The Smithsonian American Art Museum,
Washington D.C.

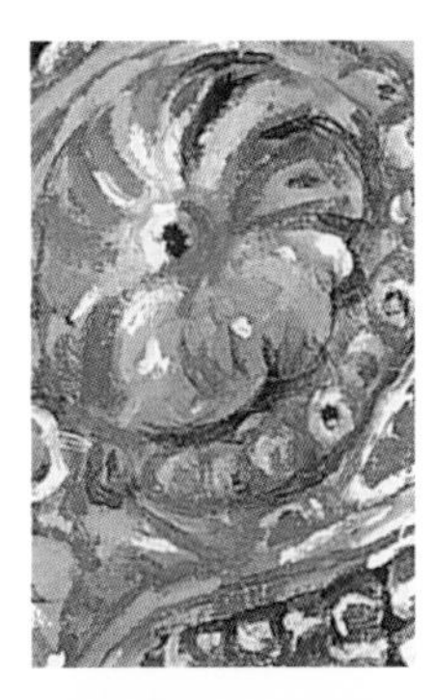

Therefore our family has been established in Pennsylvania for a long time and particularly in Pittsburgh where I was born." There was pride in the artist's words. She was always proud of her native Pittsburgh, a steel town destined to become one of the most prosperous cities in the United States. Her ancestors were among those who settled this land beginning in the 1700's, and they had many great achievements. Mary's father, Robert Simpson Cassatt (1806-1891) was a banker, although, according to her own words, he "did not have the heart of a businessman at all."

After the Bullfight

1873
Oil on canvas, 82 x 64 cm
The Art Institute of Chicago, Chicago, Illinois

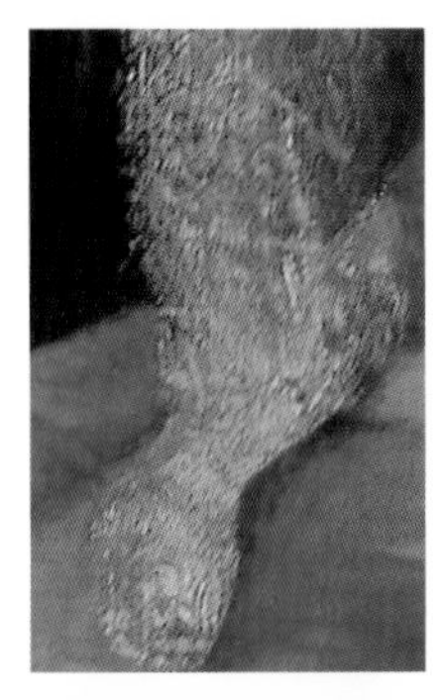

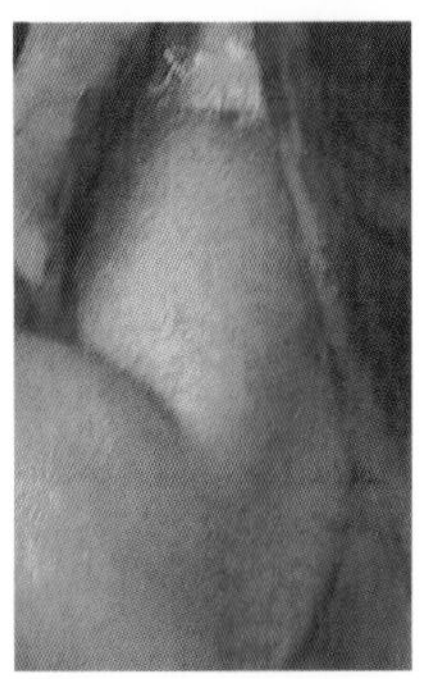

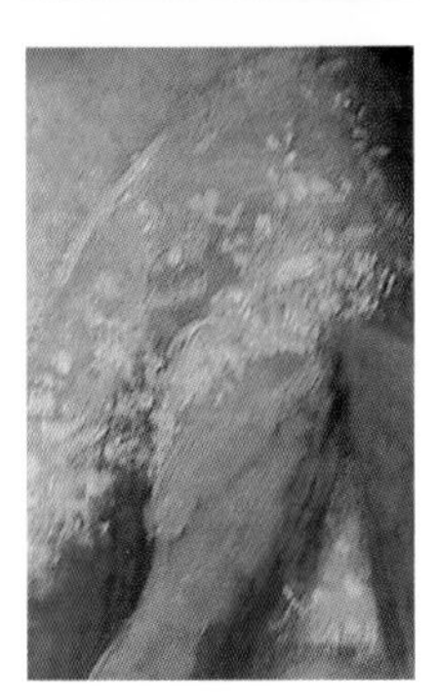

He devoted much energy to the upbringing of his children, and was successful in this as well, judging by their outstanding achievements. Mary was the fourth of his five children. Her older brother, Alexander Johnston Cassatt (1839-1906), carried on the family trade, and became president of the Pennsylvania Railroad. He was at the same time one of the main constructors of the New York Railroad and it was he who chose and implemented the plan for Central Station, which is considered to be an architectural masterpiece. As a businessman, he possessed the taste and the sophistication of a true artist. For many years, his reputation in America eclipsed the fame his sister had gained in art.

The Young Bride

1875
Oil on canvas, 87.6 x 69.9 cm
Montclair Art Museum, Montclair, New Jersey.

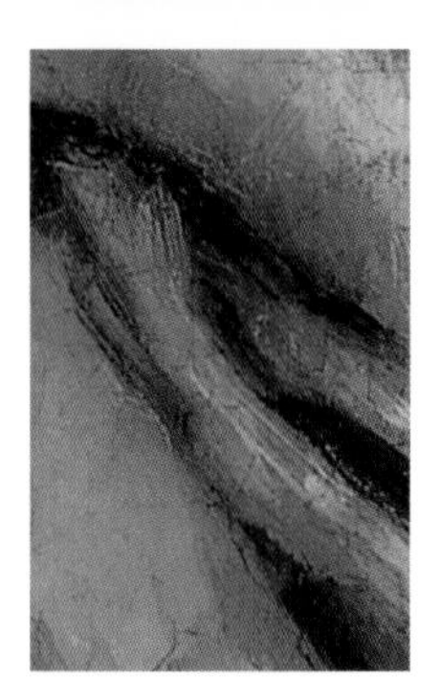

Perhaps the fact that her father "was full of French ideas", according to Mary, played a special role in his children's upbringing. That is where one more secret of the Cassatt family is revealed. It so happens that Mary's father's ancestors brought French blood into the family. "'My family is of French origin, Mary related, "Well before the Revocation of the Edict of Nantes – exactly in 1662 – a Frenchman named Cossart emigrated from France to Holland." This Cossart settled in Leyde, where many documents regarding his family are found among the records of the Walloon Church. He later moved to Amsterdam before going to settle in the United States.

Mrs Duffee Seated on a Striped Sofa, Reading

---

1876
Oil on panel, 35 x 27 cm
Boston Museum of Fine Arts, Boston, Massachusetts

M. S. Cassatt
Paris

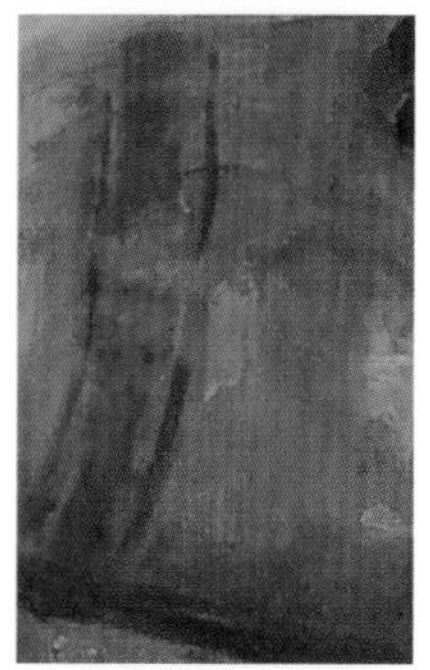

And, naturally, it was not by accident that Cossart chose New Amsterdam as his new home in that distant land. The name of this city was the thread connecting him with Europe. His grandson settled in Pennsylvania, where the family, now known as Cassatt, remained for good. Mary's father was the great-grandson of this first Pennsylvanian. However, it was not the father but the mother, Katherine Kelso Johnston (1816-1895), who nourished the yearning for the faraway, still unknown, but thrilling France in the family. The children once found in their home a letter written in flawless French by their mother at the age of twelve.

Portrait of Madame X Dressed for the Matinée

1878
Oil on canvas, 100 x 81 cm
Collection of Philip and Charles Hanes

Mary Cassatt

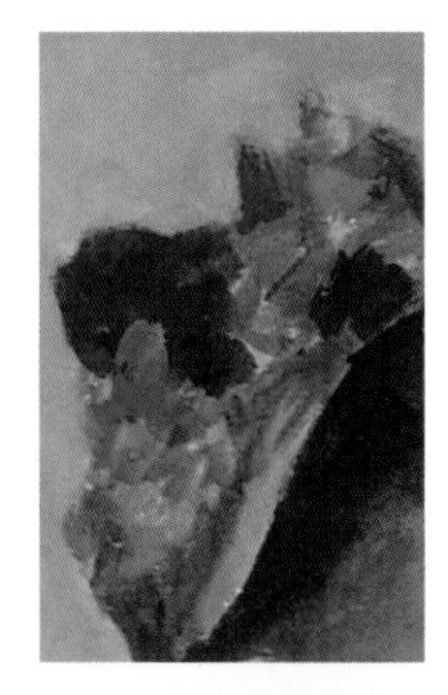

Mary had good reason to claim that "...my mother was of French culture," even though up to that point she had not yet travelled abroad. "She was partly looked after by an American lady who once lived in the boarding school of Madame Campan, an institution where there was a fairly large number of young women coming from imperial aristocracy," Mary related, "Circumstances brought this lady to Pittsburgh, where she accepted several pupils. From her my mother learned to speak perfect French and all of her life she continued corresponding in French with those of her friends who spoke this language. She was extremely knowledgeable about general culture and literature."

Portrait of the Artist

1878

Gouache on paper, 59.7 x 44.5 cm

The Metropolitan Museum of Art, New York, NY

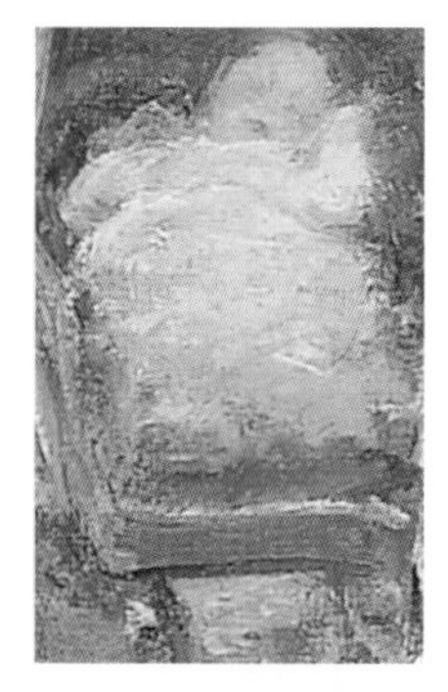

It was completely natural for this family to use any excuse for a trip to France. "The most distant of my memories is being a five or six-year-old girl, learning how to read in Paris," Mary remembered. Her parents first took her overseas in 1851 when they needed medical consultation regarding the illness of one of the children. The family remained in Europe for about five years. They not only lived in Paris, but also managed to visit other European countries. It is known, for example, that they visited Heidelberg and Darmstadt in Germany. For a child, five years is a very long time. Mary wrote and spoke in French, was immersed in a French environment,

Children in the Garden

1878
Oil on canvas, 73.6 x 92.6 cm
Collection of Mr and Mrs Meredith J. Long

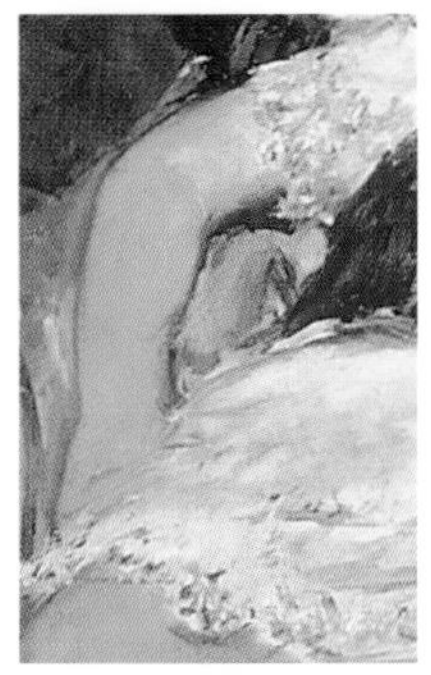

and had many unforgettable experiences. When the twelve-year-old girl returned home, she was no longer a naive, wide-eyed young American, and, possibly, her dreams about the future already involved France. In 1851, before leaving for Europe, the family moved from Pittsburgh to Philadelphia, where the children had many more educational opportunities. In 1858, fourteen-year-old Mary entered the Pennsylvania Academy of Art, which she attended for five years. Later she was able to appreciate what the school had taught her: "At the Pennsylvania Academy, we drew imitations of ancient art and antique statues," Mary recalled.

Little Girl in a Blue Armchair

1878
Oil on canvas, 89.5 x 129.8 cm
The National Gallery of Art, Washington D.C.

The schooling was probably limited to those first lessons offered by any art school. Mary was mature enough to realise the necessity of taking lessons from real professionals. In her opinion, "there was no education" at the Pennsylvania Academy. Indeed, in mid-nineteenth-century America, opportunities for artistic education were limited. In 1899, R. Mutter, one of the most renowned art historians of the nineteenth century, wrote that "until the United States declared independence (in 1776), America had neither painting nor sculpture. People ate and drank, built houses and reproduced. A piece of iron had more value than the best of statues,

Woman Reading

1878
Oil on canvas, 78.7 x 58.9 cm
Joslyn Art Museum, Omaha, Nebraska

Mary Cassatt

a yard of good fabric was preferred to Raphael's *Transfiguration."* In the United States, it was impossible to get acquainted with the paintings of old European masters since there were no collections there yet. Some of the settlers brought family portraits with them from Europe, but nothing more. "Moreover," continues Mutter, "Quakers denounced art, considering it worldly vanity. Only with time, when the dollar grew strong, did enterprising European portrait artists, who did not find luck at home, begin to appear in America.

In the Loge, at the Opera

1878
Oil on canvas, 81.2 x 66 cm
Museum of Fine Arts, Boston, Massachusetts

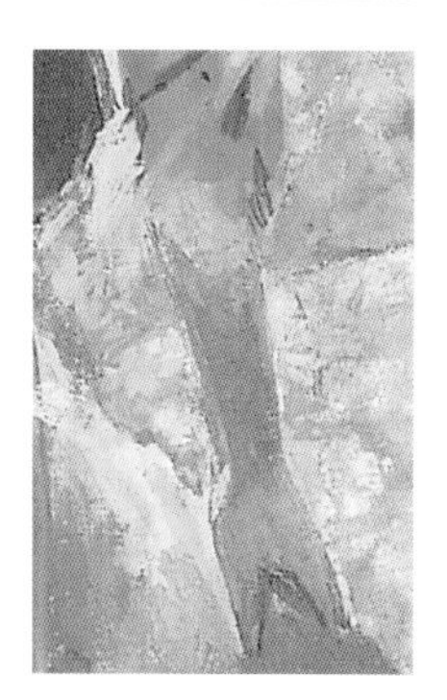

They crossed the ocean to grace the New World with their dubious works of art. " Young Americans were keenly aware that America was lagging behind the millennia-old European artistic tradition. Historians analysing the development of American art admit that in the nineteenth century it lacked the most important component: the classical background, the roots without which the most avant-garde artistic movements would never have developed. In 1864, art critic James Jackson Jarves wrote in the journal *The Art Idea* that at that moment America had "no state collections to guide a growing taste;

Woman Standing, Holding a Fan

1878-79
Distemper with metallic paint on canvas,
128.6 x 72 cm
Private Collection

no caste of persons of whom fashion demands encouragement to art growth; no ancestral homes, replete with storied portraiture of the past; no legendary lore more dignified than forest or savage life." With the booming development of American industry, only technical professions were in demand, and a technical elite began to form in big cities. Painting and drawing played merely a practical role in the new civilisation since they were used mainly for design. The times when collecting art would become not only a passion for wealthy Americans,

Woman with a Pearl Necklace in a Loge

1879
Oil on canvas, 81.3 x 59.7 cm
Philadelphia Museum of Art, Philadelphia, Pennsylvania

mary Cassatt

but also a cultural need for the country, had not yet arrived. This weakness of American culture gradually became more and more evident. The question of how to make up for this absence arose. "We buy, borrow, adopt and adapt," wrote Jarves, "For some time to come, Europe must do for us all what we are in too much of a hurry to do ourselves. It remains, then, for us to be as eclectic in our art as in the rest of our civilisations." Dozens of young Americans – for the most part men – went to England or Germany, but, naturally, most of them preferred Paris. In the mid-nineteenth century, many professors at the *École des Beaux-Arts*,

On the Balcony

1878-79
Oil on canvas, 89.9 x 65.2 cm
The Art Institute of Chicago, Chicago

members of the jury of the Annual Paris Salon, and members of European academies, had their own "free" studios in the city. Anyone could draw and paint live models there, and, for a small fee, could receive all of the same instruction as in the studios of the *École*. Young Americans were mastering techniques of classical painting. They learned the fashionable lustre of James Tissot and imitated the realism of the rebellious Courbet and even the "untidy" sketching style of young artists. When Mary entered the Philadelphia Academy, she had already chosen her career, although not without some resistance on the part of her parents.

At the Theatre

1878-79
Pastel and gouache with metallic paint
on tan wove paper, 64.6 x 54.5 cm
Private Collection

M. Cassatt

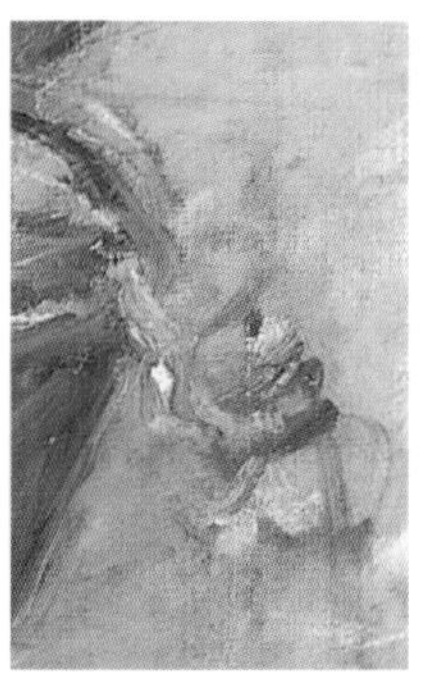

"A little before the war, so to speak around 1868, I decided to become a painter," she remembered later, "at the same time I decided to go to Europe." The choice of the European country where she would continue her studies was obvious. "Around 1868 my mother and I returned to Paris and stayed there for over a year." First of all, Mary wanted to get to know France better. The diversity of the landscape and the country's always unexpected beauty was stunning, even to its own artists. It is hard to determine the degree of Mary's interest in landscape – she later showed no interest in it.

The Cup of Tea

1879
Oil on canvas, 92.4 x 65.4 cm
The Metropolitan Museum of Art, New York, NY

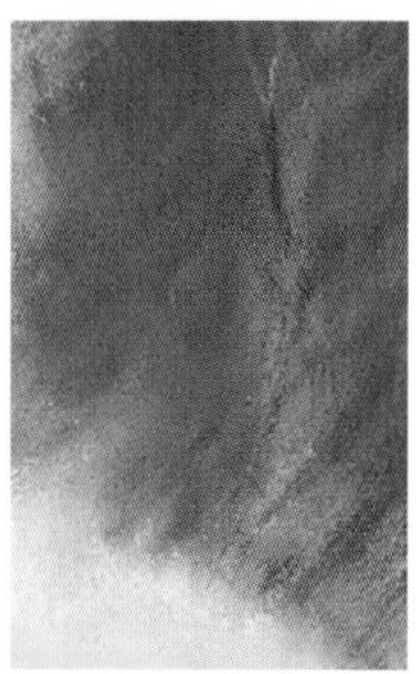

However, at the beginning of her artistic journey she needed to master everything French art had to offer. Already in the 1830's, there was a group of landscape painters who were devoting their lives to exalting the beauty and distinctive character of the French countryside. Having begun in the vicinity of Paris, in the famous Fontainebleau Forest, the "Barbizon" artists painted the fishing villages of Normandy, the woods and hills along the banks of the Seine, and the rocky shores of Brittany. By the time of Mary's arrival in France, the best masters of French landscape – Theodore Rousseau, Jules Dupré, Narcisse Diaz, Charles-François Daubigny, Camille Corot – were

## Lydia Leaning on Her Arms Seated in a Loge

1879
Pastel, 53.3 x 43.2 cm
The Nelson Gallery-Atkins Museum,
Kansas City, Missouri

not only already well-known, but had also earned an important place at the Paris Salon, and some had even joined the jury. Future Impressionists were beginning to search for a new path precisely in this genre. It is hard to imagine that the young American was not at all interested in landscape. She travelled in France for some time and then returned to the United States. America was in the midst of the Civil War at the time. Mary spent two years in Philadelphia and Chicago and then went to Europe again. The years of studying in Philadelphia had been in vain, and Mary came to a sad conclusion:

A Corner of the Loge

1879
Oil on canvas, 43.8 x 62.2 cm
Private Collection

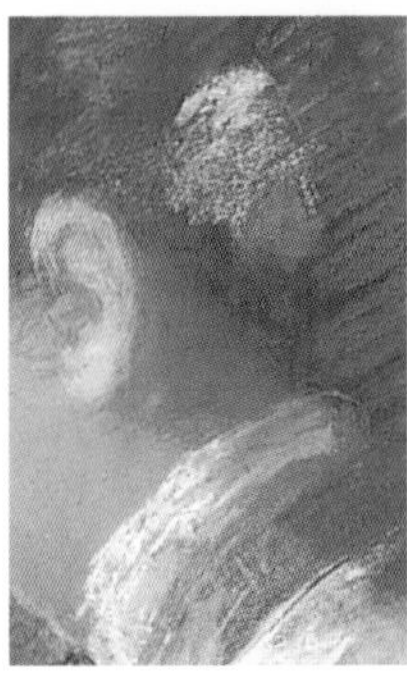

"I believe that you cannot learn painting, and that you do not need to follow the instructions of a teacher. The education of museums alone suffices." She had visited some of the European museums as a young girl. But which one to choose? Despite all of the beauty of France, there was a country in Europe where all the artists, including the French, were searching for the roots of European art. Only in Italy did they find the authentic classical art whose effect on realism became especially evident in the works of Winkelman. Medieval Italian frescos taught them to understand the harmony of colours.

At the Theatre

1879
Pastel on metallic paint on canvas, 65.1 x 81.3 cm
Philadelphia Museum of Art, Philadelphia, Pennsylvania

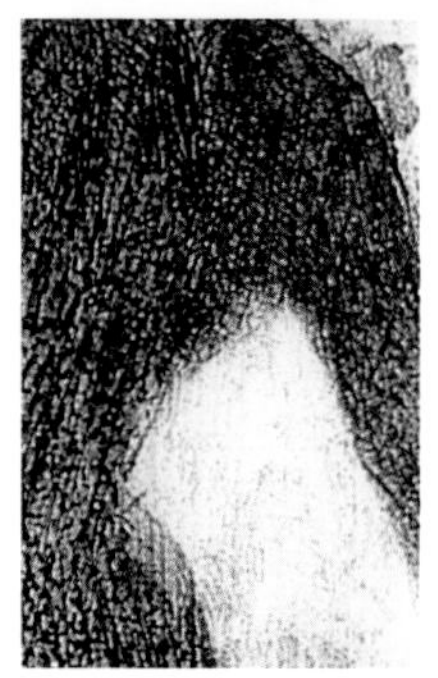

The great masters of Italian Renaissance were role models for all artists, regardless of their artistic orientation. So Mary took the path everyone else had walked before. She began in Italy. "So I left for Italy and stayed in Parma for eight months, where I entered the school of Correggio, an extraordinary master!" Mary followed in the steps of her older French contemporaries, choosing old masters. "All of his charm," Eugene Delacroix wrote of Correggio, "all his power and achievement of a genius, came from his imagination in order to awaken an echo in the imaginations created to understand it."

Interior Scene

1879
Softground etching, aquatint and drypoint on cream laid paper, 39.7 x 31 cm
National Gallery of Art, Washington D.C.

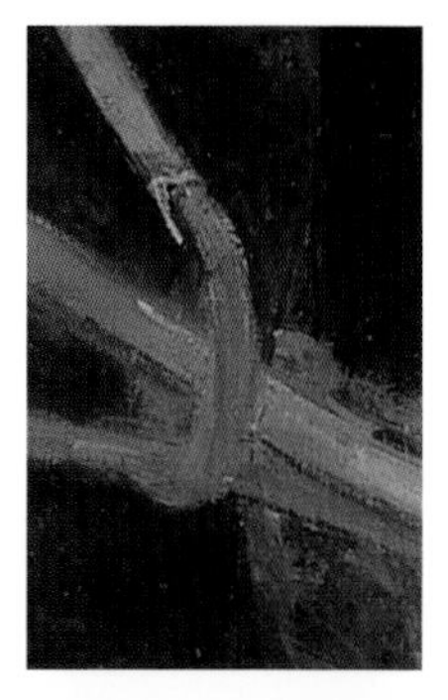

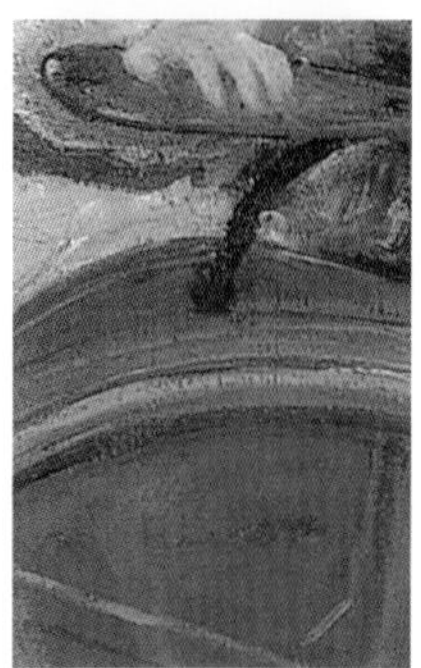

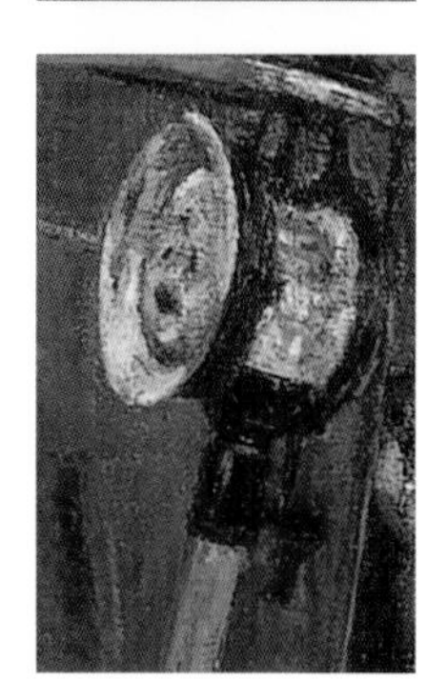

When Mary went to Parma in 1872, she was twenty-eight years old. She spent eight months there. "From there I left for Spain," Mary related, "The works of Rubens at Museo Del Prado inspired in me such admiration that I hurried from Madrid to Antwerp." It is not a bit surprising that Rubens fascinated her. In Madrid, Rome, and Antwerp, the city of Rubens, where his house still stands, Mary studied this great native of Flanders, whose art became a starting point for her French contemporaries. Delacroix called him "the most brilliant of painters". When Mary was studying the works of a master, she did so thoughtfully and consistently.

## A Woman and a Girl Driving

1881
Oil on canvas, 89.7 x 130.5 cm
The W. P. Wilstach Collection,
Philadelphia Art Museum, Philadelphia, Pennsylvania

Mary Cassatt.

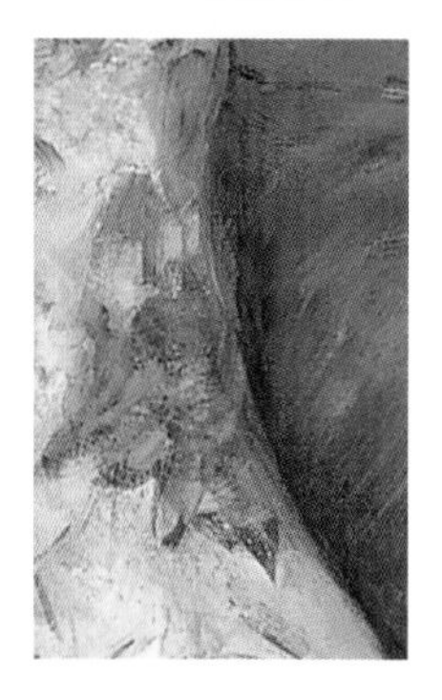

"I stayed there all summer long studying Rubens," the artist related, "It was from Rome that I returned to Paris in 1874 in order to settle there permanently". In April 1874, at 35 boulevard des Capucines, the first exhibition of the Anonymous Society of Painters, Sculptors, Printmakers, etc. took place. At that exhibition, Louis Le Roy, a critic from *Le Charivari* magazine, gave the new artists the name "Impressionists". At the time, however, Mary did not yet pay enough attention to them. Despite her somewhat ironic attitude towards art teachers, Mary followed the path of other artists, and started to look for tutors – after all, future Impressionists

The Tea

1880

Oil on canvas, 64.7 x 92 cm

Maria Hopkins Fund, Museum of Fine Arts, Boston

Mary Cassatt

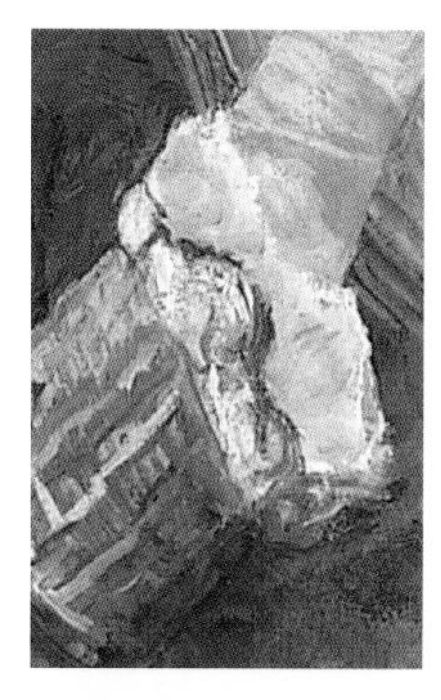

spent time at the studio of Professor Charles Glaire! But how to choose a teacher? Perhaps her choice in this matter was not original either. It is known that already during her stay in Paris in 1866 she had taken private lessons from Jean-Léon Gérôme. Gérôme's very name was almost synonymous with academic painting. A professor at the *École des Beaux-Arts*, a member of thirteen European academies, Gerome was always the star of the Paris Salon. He was able to adapt to any taste of the *nouveaux-riches*, the main purchasers of salon art. Mary spent only a short time studying under his guidance, although perhaps he, too, contributed to perfecting her artistic skill.

Lydia Crocheting in the Garden at Marly

1880
Oil on canvas, 65.6 x 92.6 cm
The Metropolitan Museum of Art, New York, NY

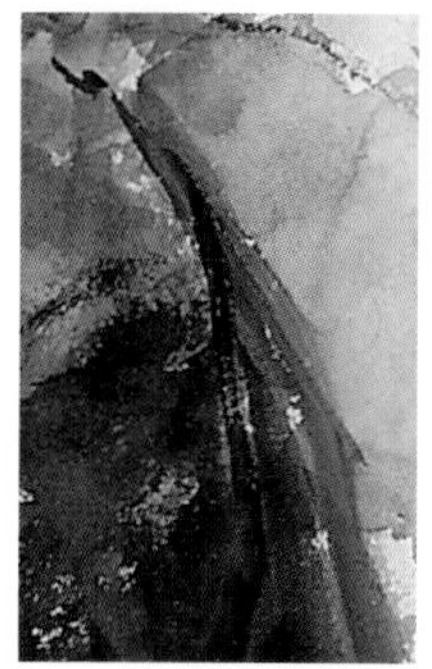

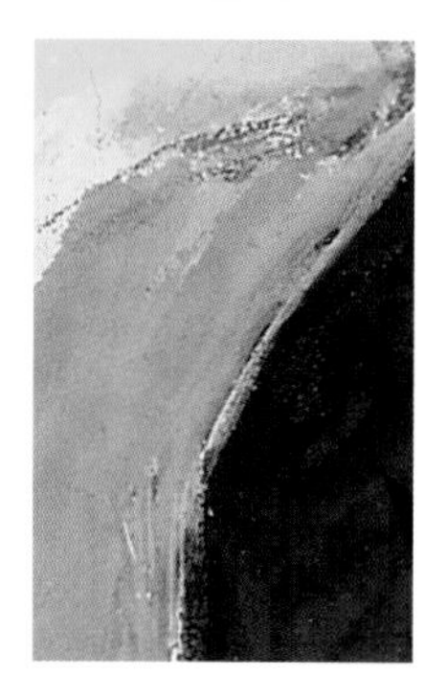

Having returned to France in 1867, she studied for a while at the artistic communes in Courances and Écouen, together with her friend from the Philadelphia Academy, Elisa Haldeman. Thomas Couture, a professor of Édouard Manet, was among her teachers. If, however, one tries to find a distinct influence of one of her mentors in her art, it is more likely to be Charles Chaplin. It is not clear whose recommendation she followed, but it was not surprising that the young woman came to study in the atelier of Charles Chaplin. Chaplin, too, was one of the professors at the *École des Beaux-Arts*. He was known as a painter, a superb sketcher, and a lithographer.

Self Portrait

1880

Watercolour on ivory wove paper, 83.8 x 61 cm
National Portrait Gallery, Washington D.C.

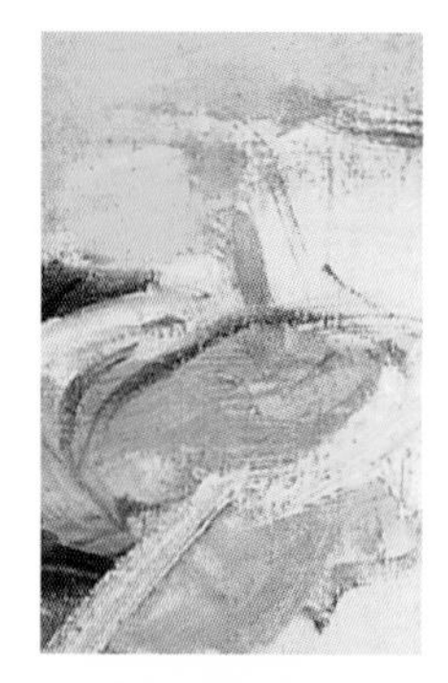

His pictures were exhibited at the Salon every year, and, along with a few other chosen ones, were reprinted in large Salon albums. Those few women who studied at the *École des Beaux-Arts* specifically chose Chaplin, since he was rightly regarded as a painter of feminine themes. Eva Gonzalès, a daughter of a famous Parisian writer and a future student of Édouard Manet, was for a while one of Chaplin's students as well. Chaplin used artistic techniques appropriate for the representation of women. "In the works of Charles Chaplin, Fragonard was reborn," wrote Mutter, "He is a master of

Portrait of Alexander J. Cassatt

1880
Oil on canvas, 64.5 x 90.7 cm
Detroit Institute of Arts, Detroit, Michigan

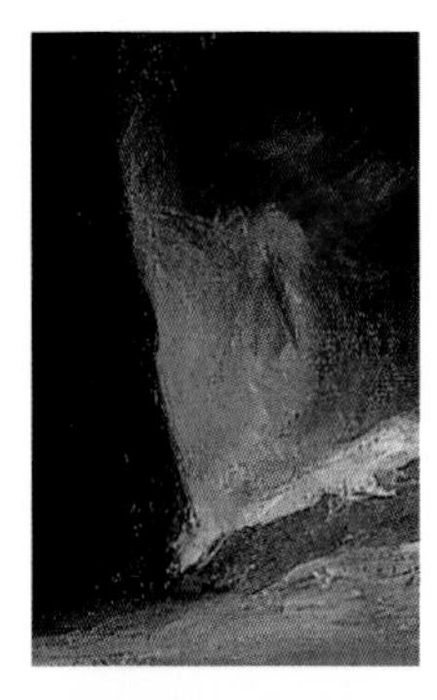

sultry bodies and rice powder, a subtle portrayer of aristocratic beauty, his palette preserved the glamour of the *fêtes galantes* of the eighteenth century. Chaplin represented dreamy, sensual women, and his paintings impressed observers with their grace, elegance, and beauty. Chaplin inherited Fragonard's refined colours and sensuality. "None of the French painters since the Rococo period can compare with him in the ability to paint hairstyles, beauty marks, chin dimples, shoulders, and breasts. Spring and falling rose petals, young girls, buds *à la Greuse*, wilting beauties,

Miss Mary Ellison

1880
Oil on canvas, 85.5 x 65.1 cm
The Chester Dale Collection,
The National Gallery of Art, Washington D.C.

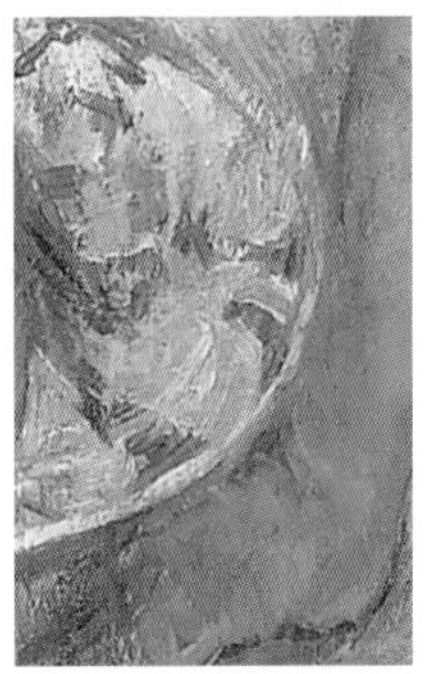

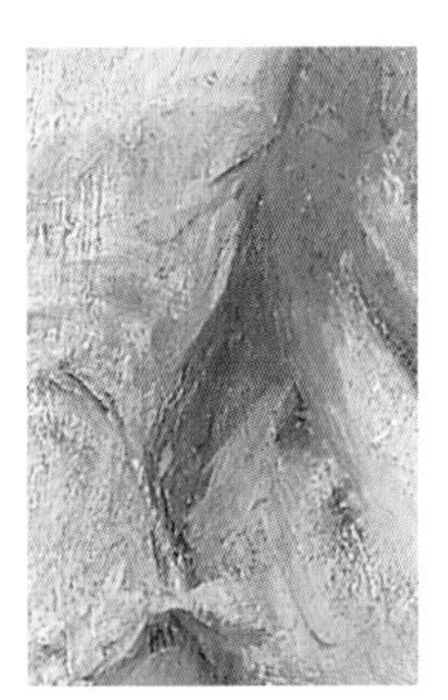

whose aroma is all the more delicious – all these were elements which formed his refined and depraved and yet light-hearted art." Chaplin possessed yet another quality of a Rococo painter – he was a first-class decorator. In 1857, he decorated the Flower Hall in Turilli, in 1881-1865 the Empress's bathroom at the Élysée Palace, and, in 1865, a number of private residences in Paris, Brussels and New York. It is possible that Mary had already heard his name back in America. "This graceful and superficial art was always liked by those who don't like painting," wrote the critic Ségard.

Mother About to Wash Her Sleepy Child

1880
Oil on canvas, 100.2 x 65.7 cm
Los Angeles County Museum of Art, California

Young people laughed at Chaplin's sentimental paintings, but one could not fail to appreciate his free style and the harmony of his palette. Édouard Manet valued the freedom of his art. "My works submitted to the Salon preceded my appearance there in person," remembered Mary. Indeed, the artist had already submitted her work to the Salon for the first time in 1868, under the pseudonym Mary Stevenson. *Mandolin Player* resembled seventeenth-century Italian paintings most of all. The effect of light on the dark background is reminiscent of Caravaggio.

Autumn

1880
Oil on canvas, 93 x 65 cm
Petit Palais - Musée des Beaux-Arts de la ville de Paris, Paris

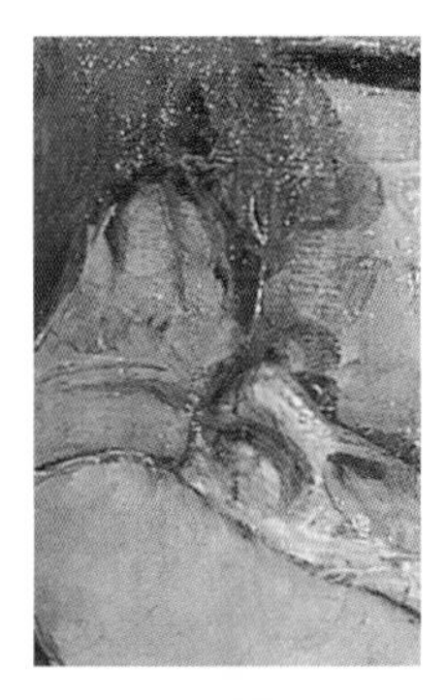

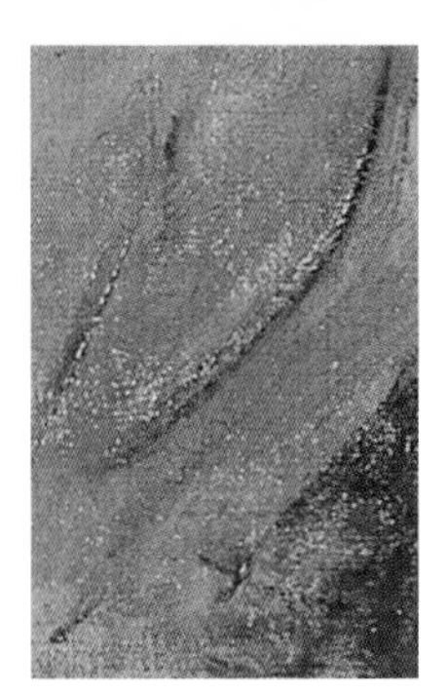

The painting was still fairly naive, although the jury's high mark must have been a tribute to her professional qualities. In 1869, Mary was refused, but in the next year, 1870, her painting *A Peasant Woman from Fobello, Sesia Valley (Piemont)* was accepted again. When the Franco-Prussian war began, Mary left for Philadelphia. In America, she exhibited her pictures in New York and Chicago. Her own memories about participation in the Salon date from the time of her return to Europe after the war. "My first picture – in 1872 – represented two women throwing candy on the day of the Carnival.

Susan Comforting the Baby (No. 1)

1881
Oil on canvas, 43.2 x 58.4cm
Columbus Museum of Arts, Columbus, Ohio

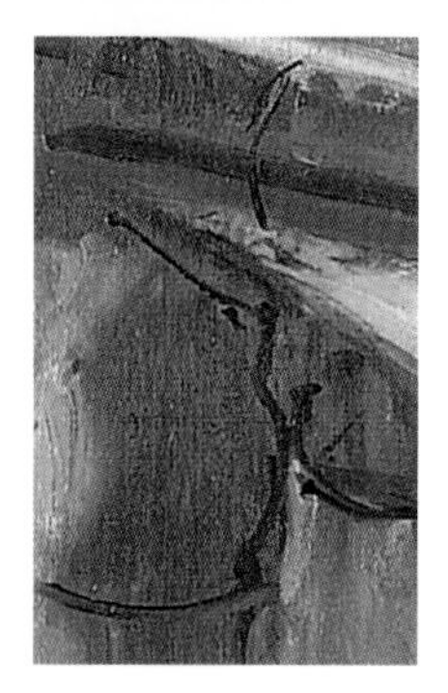

I painted it in Parma. The influence of Correggio was evident." The painting was called *On a Balcony* (p.15) and was "Spanish", as Spanish art is imagined outside Spain. This may have been the expression of her dream of a beautiful country she had not yet visited. The fairly contrived, albeit highly professionally-constructed composition reminds one more of Murillo than Correggio. In 1873, Mary spent almost seven months in Seville, where she especially fell in love with the works of Murillo.

## Lydia Working at a Tapestry Frame

1881
Oil on canvas, 63.5 x 91.4 cm
Gift of the Whiting Foundation,
Flint Institute of Arts, Flint, Michigan

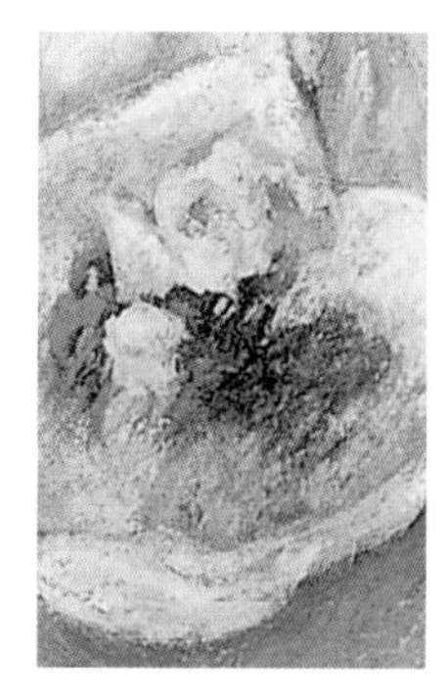

Her admiration of Spanish art found its expression in yet another painting, *Offering the Panal to the Bullfighter* (p. 13), which was also accepted by the Salon. "The second of my pictures submitted to the Salon was accepted in 1873," remembered the artist, "It represented a *torero* to whom a young girl offers a glass of water." Mary Cassatt had as much luck with the Salon as the young Parisians she later met in the circle of Impressionists did. In the late sixties and early seventies, paintings by Monet, Pissarro,

Women in a Loge

1881-82
Pastel with gouache over softground etching and aquatint on off-white paper, 29 x 22 cm
Cincinnati Art Museum, Cincinnati, Ohio

Renoir, Sisley, and Berthe Morisot were sometimes accepted, one or so a year, and sometimes rejected. Experienced artists of the older generation, such as Corot and Courbet, were by then used to submitting their most polished paintings. The young generation had a more aggressive attitude towards the jury. They did not try to adjust their works to please its members, but instead tried to have their art accepted as it was. Cézanne was openly trying to put the jury in an uncomfortable position – his friend Zola believed that this approach could only assure that in the next ten years his works would be rejected every single time.

Two Young Ladies in a Loge

1882
Oil on canvas, 79.8 x 63.8 cm
The National Gallery of Art, Washington D.C.

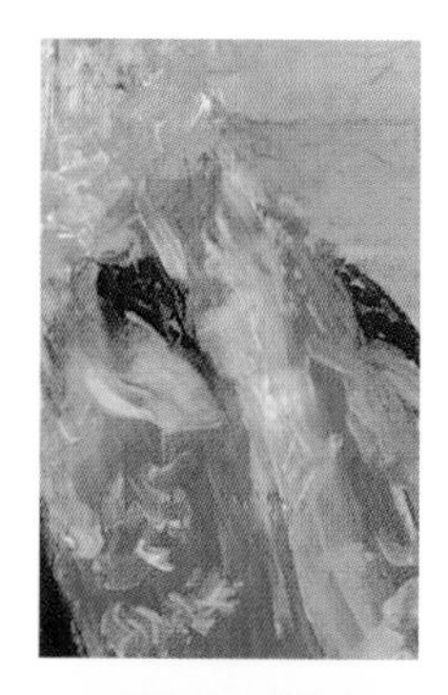

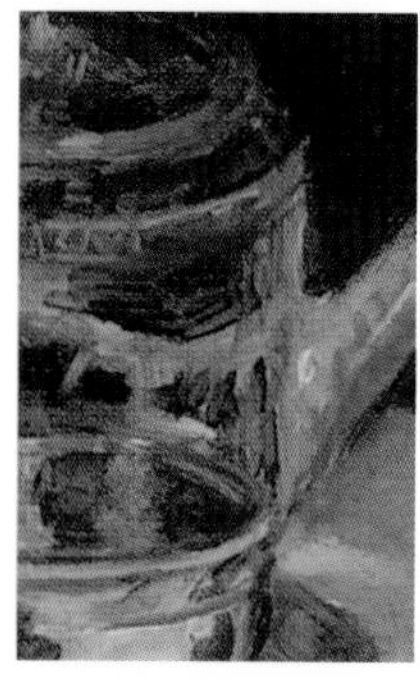

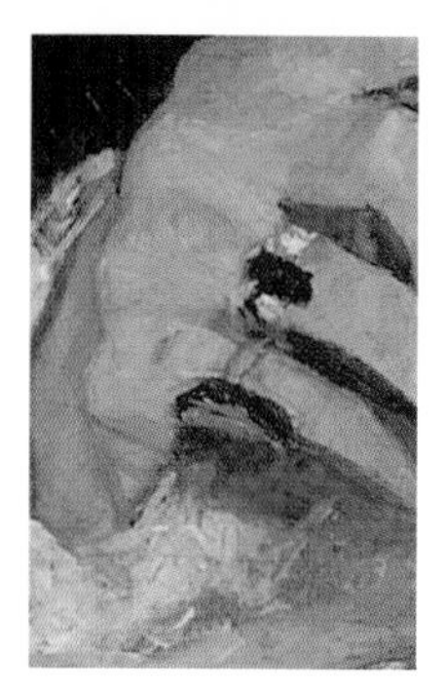

Frédéric Basille, who was at the time a leader of the group of artists who came to be known as Impressionists, wrote that the jury was unanimous in their hostility towards Impressionists. This is understandable since among the members there were such zealous defenders of the classical tradition as Cabanel and Gérôme. The few supporters of the new genre, such as landscape painters Daubigny and Corot, could not stand up to them. In 1870, Daubigny was not able to persuade the jury to accept even one of Monet's paintings. And when in 1874 the Impressionists were thinking of organising their own, separate exhibition,

Lady at the Tea Table

1883-85
Oil on canvas, 73.7 x 61 cm
The Metropolitan Museum of Art, New York, NY

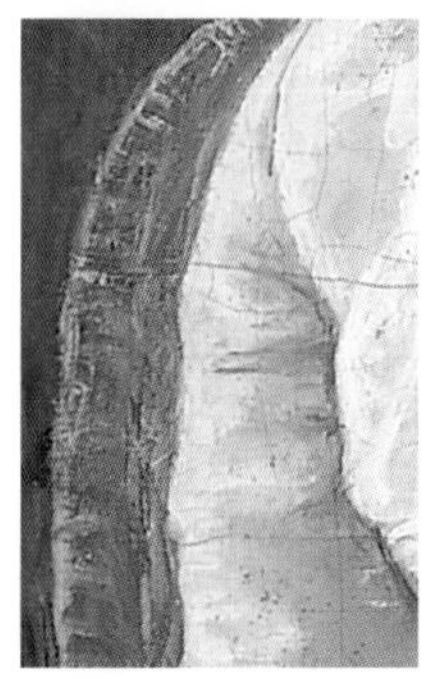

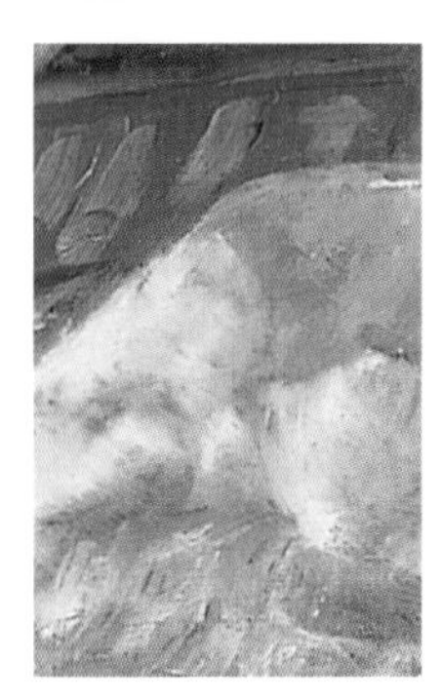

the main obstacle was still the ambiguity of how to relate to the Salon – whether to struggle for its acceptance or oppose its conventions. It was on this question that they disagreed with Édouard Manet. The artists deliberately opened their first exhibition two weeks prior to the official opening of the Salon, April 15th 1874, so that no one would suspect them of organising the show because they had been rejected by the Salon. Meanwhile, Mary kept submitting paintings to the Salon every year, and, according to her own words, quite successfully: "In 1874, a head of a young girl with hair almost red, painted in Rome under the influence

Young Girl at a Window

1883
Oil on canvas, 101.6 x 64.8 cm
Corcoran Gallery of Art, Washington D.C.

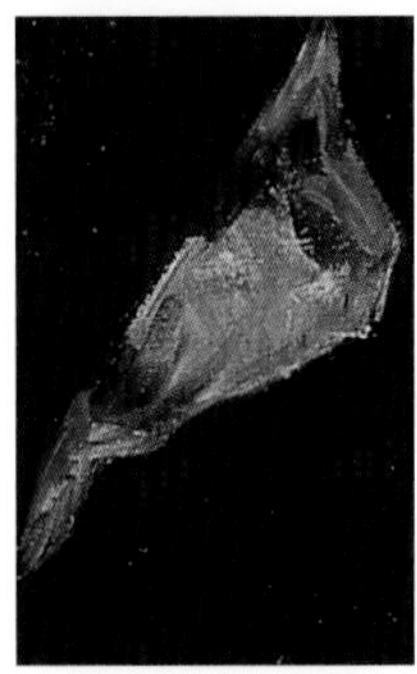

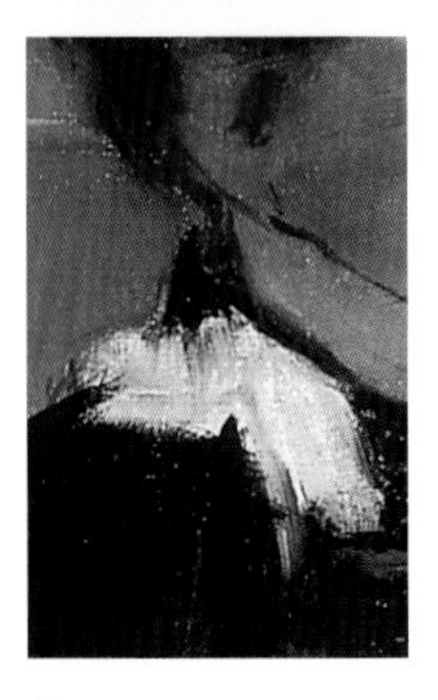

of Rubens, was noticed by several people whose opinion was not without importance." It was possibly this very portrait that attracted the attention of Degas. And unsurprisingly so: the sincere, albeit somewhat naive work of the young American presented a sharp contrast to the compositions surrounding it at the Salon. Her portrait did not fit into the characteristic repertoire of the time, where scenes from Roman life hung next to bloody dramas set in oriental harems, Hercules, Roland and Don Juan competed with François I and Louis XVI, young girls of Herzegovina with brides of Alsace. The established masters of the Salon—Gustave Boulanger, Fernand Cormon, Jules Breton,

Young Woman in Black (Portrait of Madame J.)

1883
Oil on canvas, 78.7 x 64.8
The Robert Gilmor, Jr. Collection,
Courtesy of the Baltimore Museum,
The Peabody Institute, Baltimore, Maryland.

and others—gave their outdated romantic paintings the degree of sentimentality, vulgarity, and, frequently, obscenity that satisfied the taste of potential Salon visitors coming to purchase art. As for contemporary life, it was reflected in pictures of heart-warming peasant women and fishermen's wives, awaiting the return of their husbands atop the cliffs. Even the very elegant Paris street scenes painted by De Nittis, a friend of Degas who also exhibited his work with Impressionists, seemed natural in comparison. As for Mary's teacher, Charles Chaplin, his sensual beauties constantly attracted a certain circle of admirers.

Children Playing on the Beach

1884
Oil on canvas, 97.4 x 74.2 cm
The National Gallery of Art, Washington D.C.

Mary Cassatt

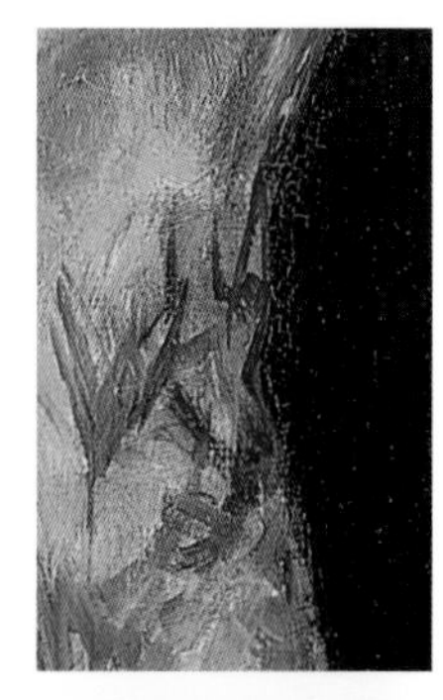

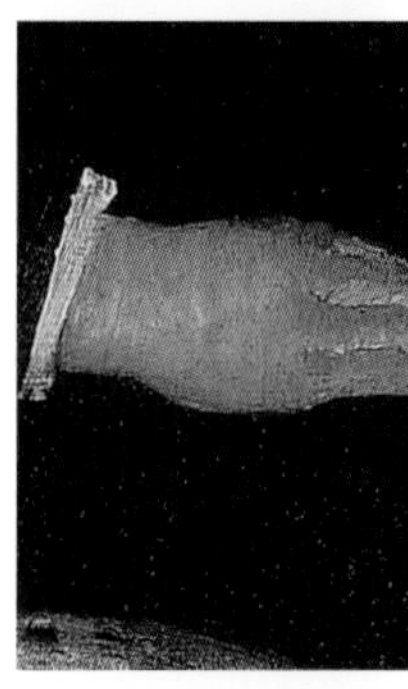

In the 1875 Salon album of reproductions published by Goupil, there was a reproduction of Chaplin's typical painting called *Roses de Mai* (Roses of May). It portrayed a bare-breasted young woman with a fan in her hand contemplating a rose lying on top of a pearl necklace. The picture was accompanied by the following sonnet:

"Déjà la fauvette et l'abeille
Voltigent dans l'air embaumé ;
Déjà le printemps ensoleille
Les nouvelles roses de mai ;
Mignonne, ouvre enfin ton oreille
Au soufflé aimant, au soffle aimé ;

Portrait of Alexander J. Cassatt
and His Son Robert Kelso Cassatt

1884
Oil on canvas, 100.3 x 81.3 cm
Philadelphia Art Museum, Philadelphia, Pennsylvania

Écoute, en ton Coeur qui s'éveille,
Bourdonner l'amour enfermé !"

(Already songbird and bee/Flutter in the fragrant air/Already the spring sun shines/Upon new roses of May/Sweetheart, listen at last/To an awestruck lover, to whispers of love/Listen, in your awakening heart/Buzzes imprisoned love). Mary submitted portraits of her relatives to the Salon, especially of her sister, Lydia, pictures of women indoors or with a landscape in the background. Her pictures had neither exoticism, nor the witticisms fashionable in the Salon, nor sentimentality, nor the usual set of roses, silk, and pearls.

Jenny Cassatt and Her Son

1885
Oil on canvas, 71.1 x 61 cm
The Newark Museum, Newark, New Jersey

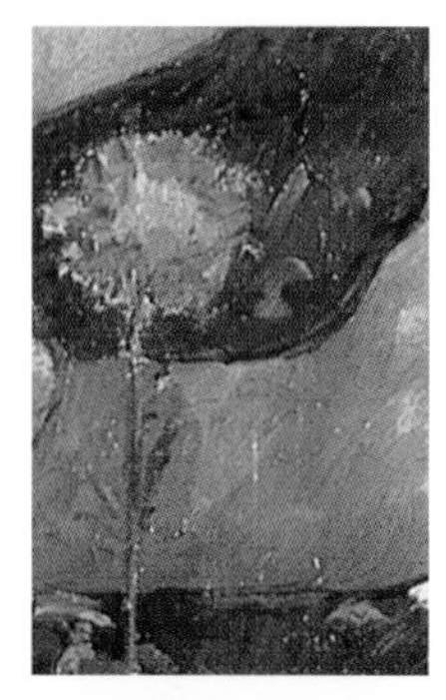

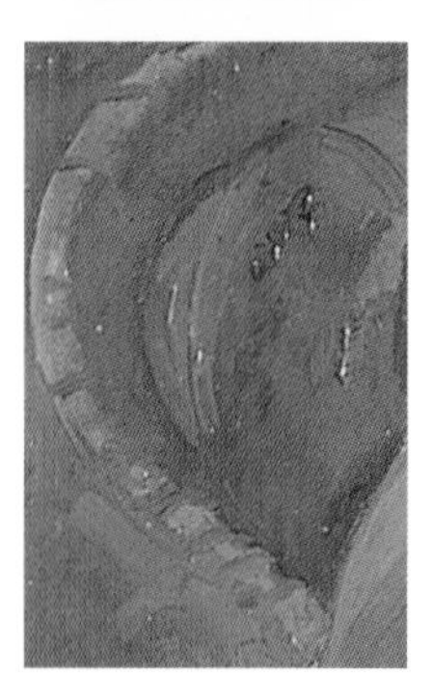

Her characters were unsophisticated, taken directly from everyday life, and naturally her pictures were frequently overlooked. Nevertheless, Mary was determined: "In 1875, they refused to accept a portrait of my sister standing, painted in front of a light background. I believed that I guessed correctly the reason for the refusal and darkened the background. The following year the same portrait was accepted. In 1877, I made another submission. It was refused. It was at that time that Degas got me to not submit any more pictures to the Salon, but instead to show them together with a group of impressionists."

The Family

1886
Oil on canvas, 81.3 x 67.3 cm
Gift of Walter P. Chrysler, Jr;
The Chrysler Museum, Norfolk, Virginia

Mary Cassatt

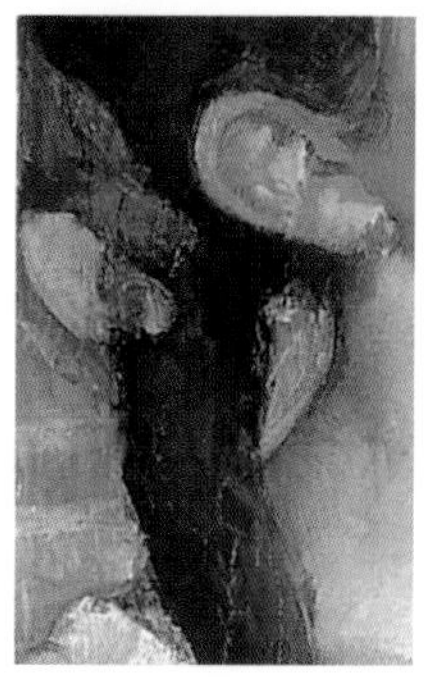

It is hard to tell how Degas and Cassatt met. According to some biographers, Mary met an artist named Tourny, a friend of Degas, in Antwerp. "They [Degas and Tourney] were together at the 1874 Salon," writes Ségard, "Tourny led Degas to a portrait of a young woman, painted by Mary Cassatt while in Rome. Degas stopped and said 'It is true. Here is someone who feels things as I do.'" Later, Jones Revald, a friend of Degas, visited Mary's studio, perhaps together with Tourny. Around the same time, between 1874 and 1876, Degas wrote a letter to his friend James Tissot in London (the letter is not dated):

Girl Arranging Her Hair

1886
Oil on canvas, 75.1 x 62.5 cm
The National Gallery of Art, Washington D.C.

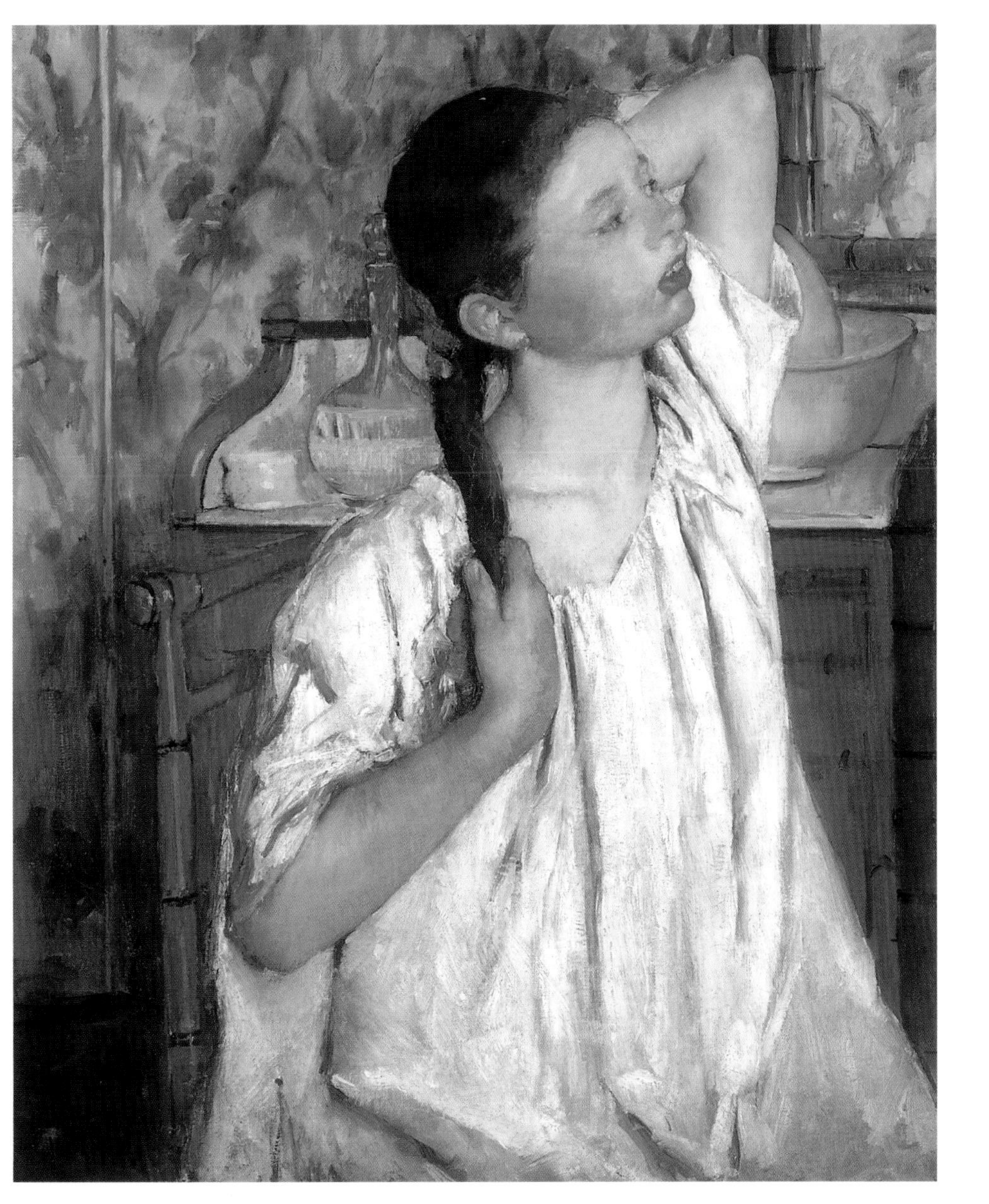

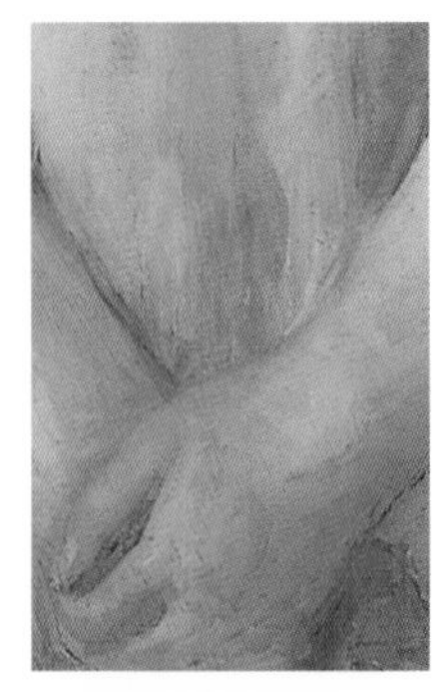

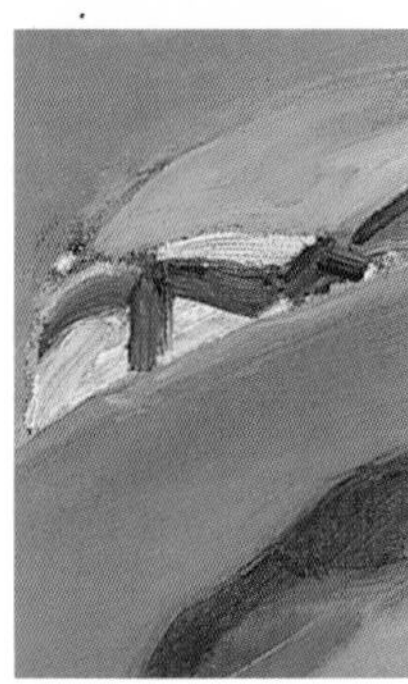

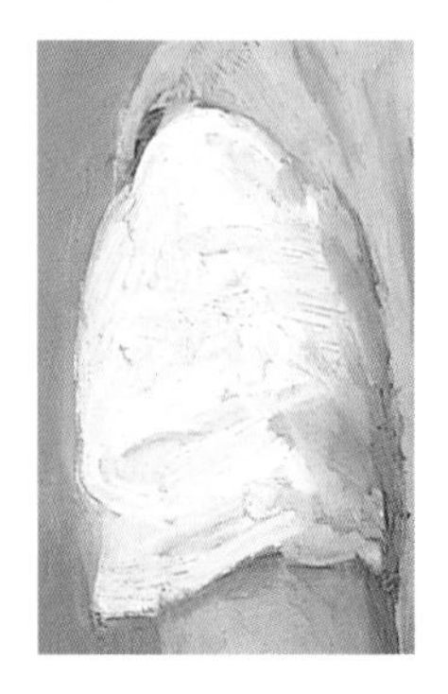

"My dear Tissot,

You have recommended the two Americans to me in a fairly vague manner. Several days ago, I went to see them. One, it seemed, was not feeling well since her arrival. Also, the weather that befell them upon their coming here prevented them from going out more often. They don't know yet if they are going to stay in Paris. Who are they? How did you get to know them? Bowles (an editor, a friend of Tissot–N.B.) met them on a train. They were accompanied by a brother who was neither mentioned or introduced to me here. How can they expect to take lessons in comedy or drama speaking so little French? How do you want me to help them?

Little Girl in a Big Straw Hat and Pinafore

1886
Oil on canvas, 65.3 x 49.2 cm
The National Gallery of Art, Washington D.C.

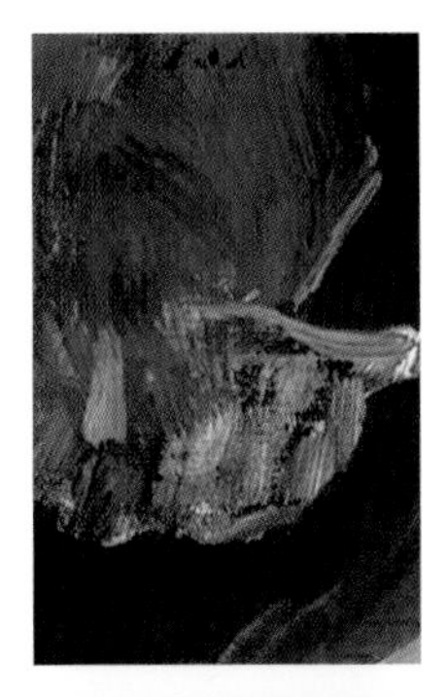

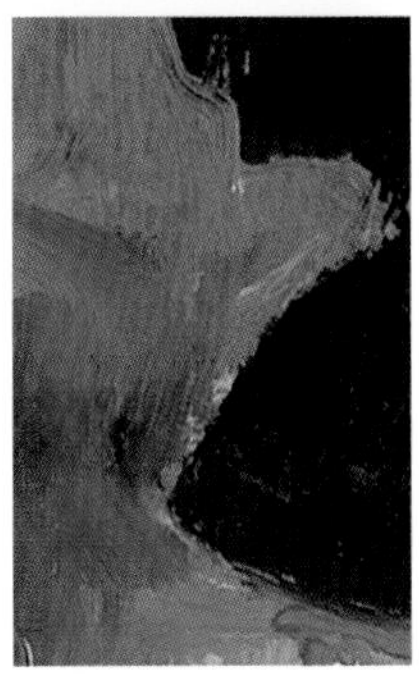

It's always a question of money, and I don't have an excess of it. You have surely promised them on my behalf much more than I can provide. You, therefore, did them a disservice." Perhaps Mary was accompanied by her sister, Lydia, who often visited France, and in 1877 had permanently moved to Paris with their parents. It is surprising that Degas describes the Americans as speaking little French and wanting to take acting lessons. In any case, the painter Tissot referred them specifically to Degas. Sometime during this period Degas saw Mary's works at the Salon and liked them

Young Woman Sewing in a Garden

1886
Oil on canvas, 91.4 x 64.8 cm
Antonin Personnaz Collection,
Musée d'Orsay, Paris

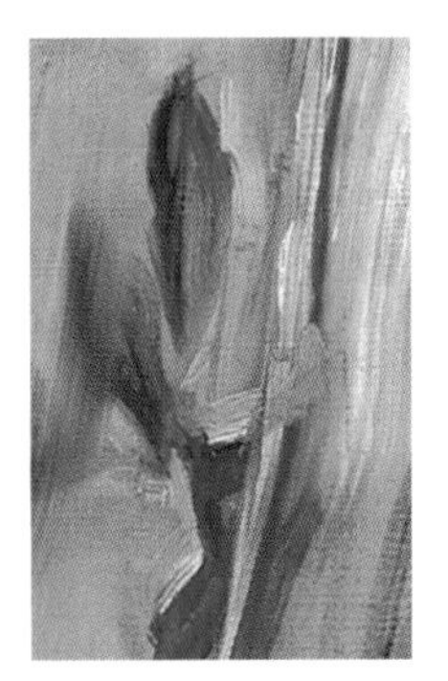

very much, inviting her to show her works together with the Impressionists. "I accepted this offer with joy," she recalled, "I could finally work with absolute independence, without worrying about the eventual opinion of the jury! By then I already knew the real character of my venerable mentors." Degas' invitation was not entirely a surprise. By that time, she had already formed her preferences regarding contemporary French art. "I admired Manet, Courbet, and Degas. I hated conventional art. I began to live..." Her new life began at the Impressionists' Fourth Exhibition.

Portrait of an Elderly Lady

1887
Oil on canvas, 72.9 x 60.3 cm
The National Gallery of Art, Washington D.C.

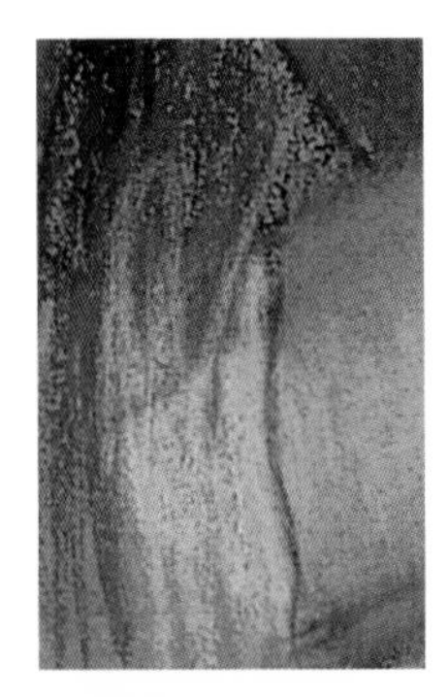

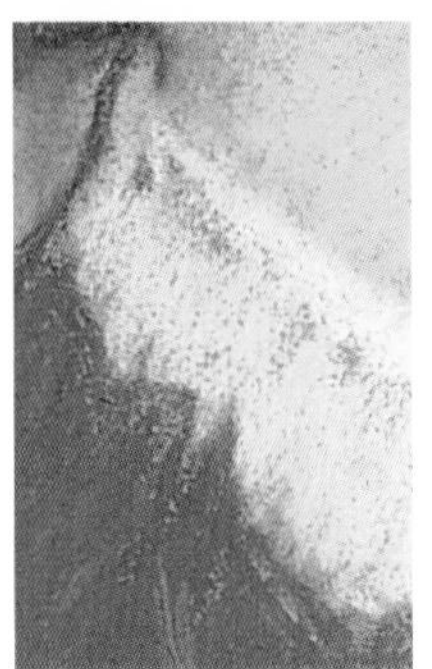

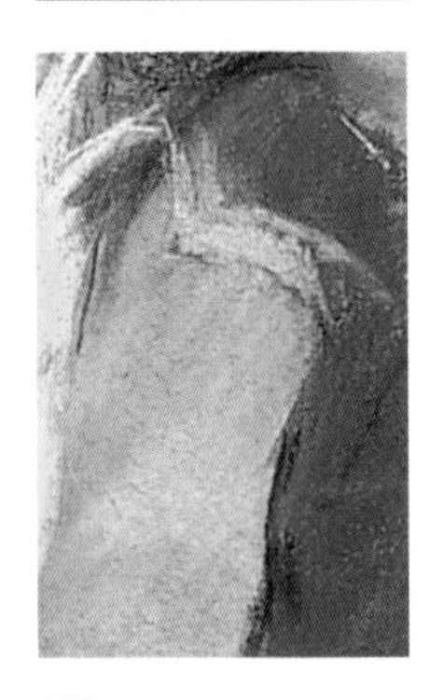

The Fourth Exhibition opened on April 10th 1897 in a rented apartment on the second floor at 28 avenue de l'Opéra and was called "The Exposition of Independent Artists". From the very beginning, Degas did not like the name "the Impressionists", and this time was able to insist on changing it. The critic Leroy – the godfather of the Impressionists – a journalist who in 1874 published his famous article "The Impressionist Show" in *Le Charivari*, regretted that the participating artists traded such a notable name for the indefinite and meaningless "independent". Armand Silvestre, the advocate of impressionism, wrote that although the name

Young Mother

1888

Pastel on tan wove paper, 84 x 73.8 cm
The Art Institute of Chicago, Illinois.

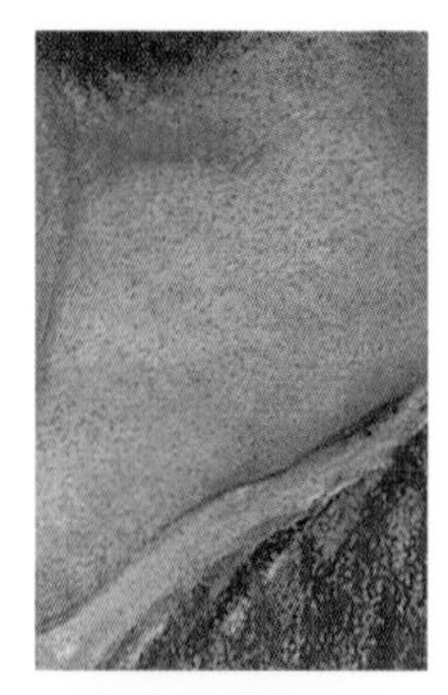

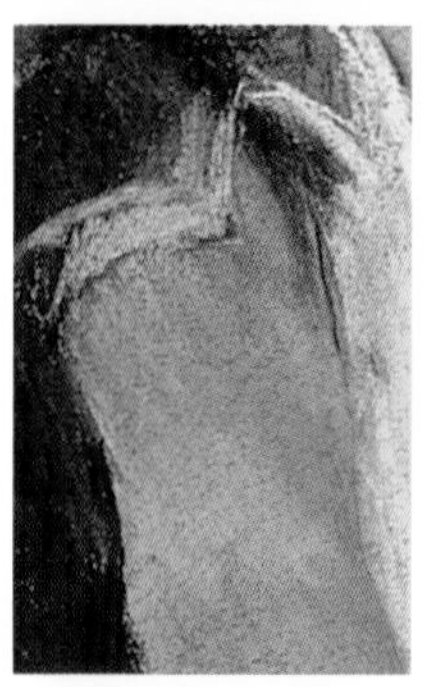

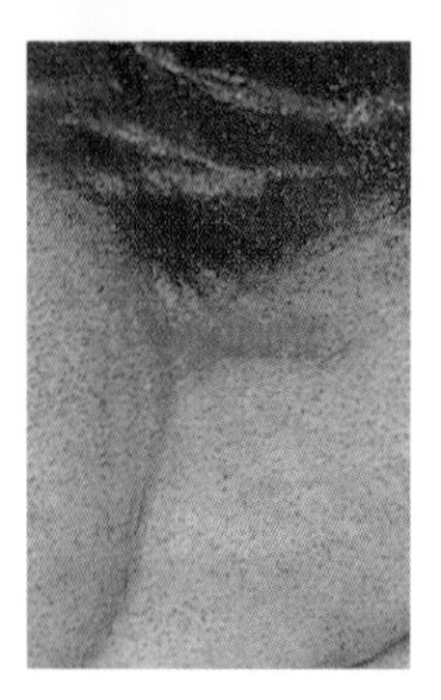

had changed, the substance of the genre remained. By that time, the group had seen member turnover as well. Monet, whose painting *Impression, Soleil Levant* (Impression, Sunrise), gave the genre its name, still participated in the show. Renoir, Sisley, Cézanne, and Guillaumin, however, decided to try the Salon instead, and Berthe Morisot was pregnant. Degas found himself the leader of the society. He filled in the gaps with his protégés – Mary Cassatt, Louis Forain, François Somier, and Federico Zandomeneghi, who presented many paintings. Following a dark hall with watercolours by the late artist Piette, and the next one, exhibiting Marie Bracquemond's

Mother's Goodnight Kiss

1888
Pastel, 83.8 x 73.7 cm
Potter Palmer Collection,
The Art Institute Chicago, Illinois.

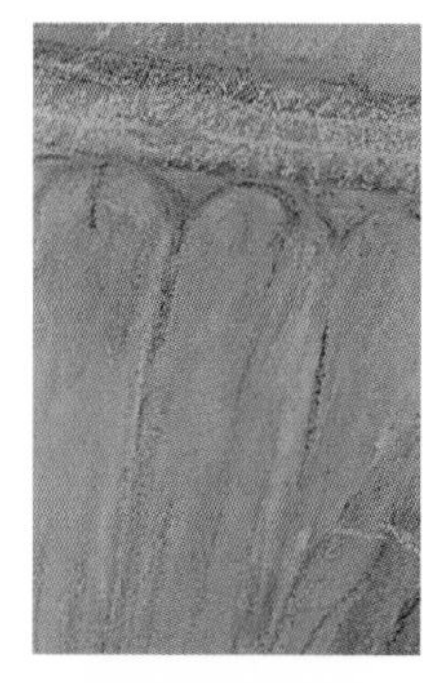

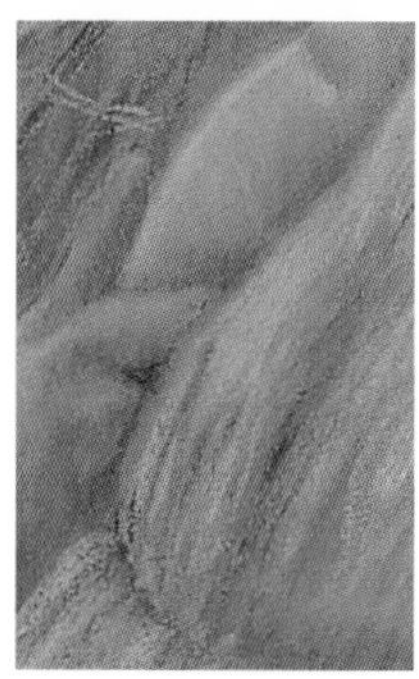

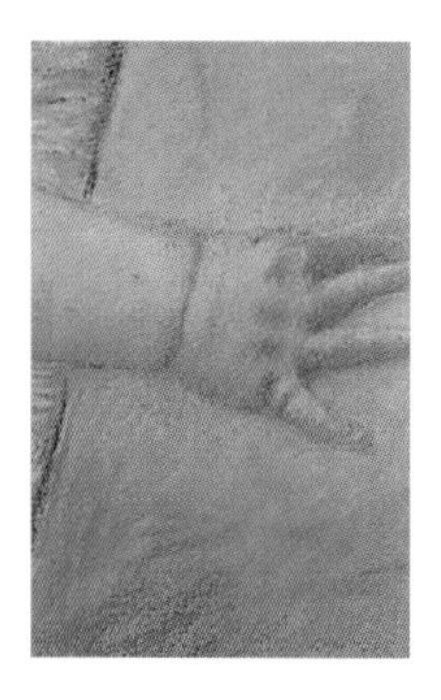

large decorative panels and paintings by Degas and Forain, there was a third hall, with the works of Caillebotte and Mary Cassatt. Mary presented twelve pictures in oil, tempera, and pastel. By now, she had already declared her choice of subject, which remained unchanged throughout all of her artistic career – pictures of women and children. One of the paintings – *Woman Reading* (p. 33) – was especially notable. This picture was purchased by Antonin Proust, a friend of Édouard Manet. Four pictures portrayed women against the background of a theatre hall,

Mother Holding a Baby Who Reaches Out to the Right

1889
Pastel on tan wove paper, 73 x 60 cm
Ursula and R. Stanley Johnson Family Collection, Illinois

Mary Cassatt

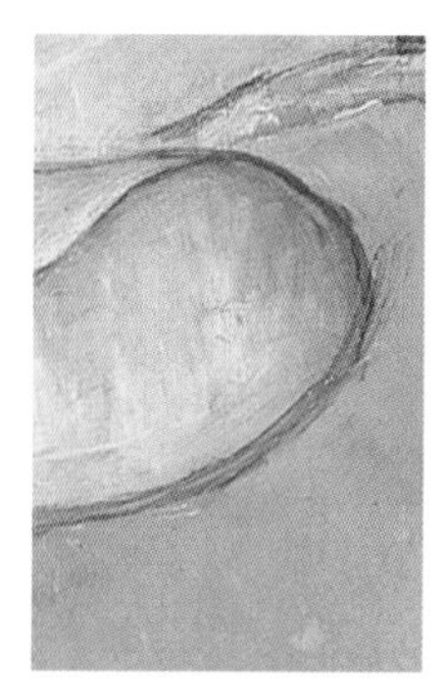

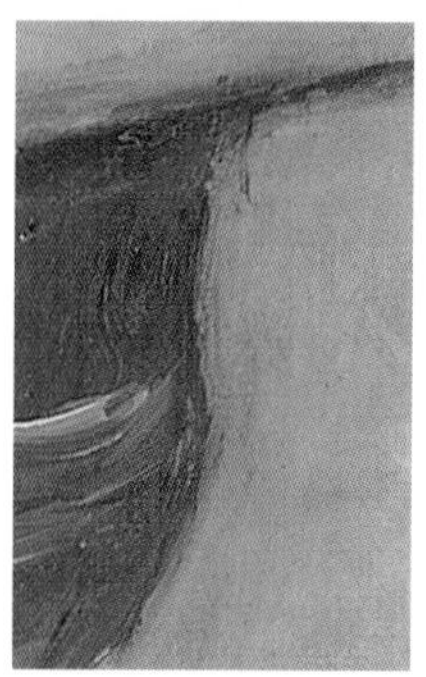

undoubtedly painted under the influence of Renoir, although, according to an American biographer, Mary Cassatt "had reservations about Renoir, whom she considered too sensual". At the show, Mary's pictures stood out with their brightly painted frames, demonstrating the young artists' protest against the traditional, "bourgeois" custom of coating picture frames in gold. Following her example, Pissarro, too, painted his frames for the subsequent Fifth Exhibition, and, after him, in the 1880s, the pointillist Seurat made it his practice as well. At the 1879 show, Cassatt's picture Study:

Mother and Child

1889
Oil on canvas, 73.2 x 59.8 cm
John J. Emery Endowment, Cincinnati Art Museum
Cincinnati, Ohio

Mary Cassatt

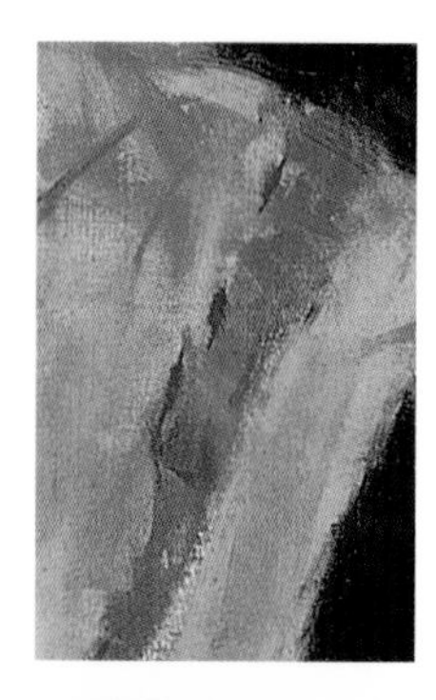

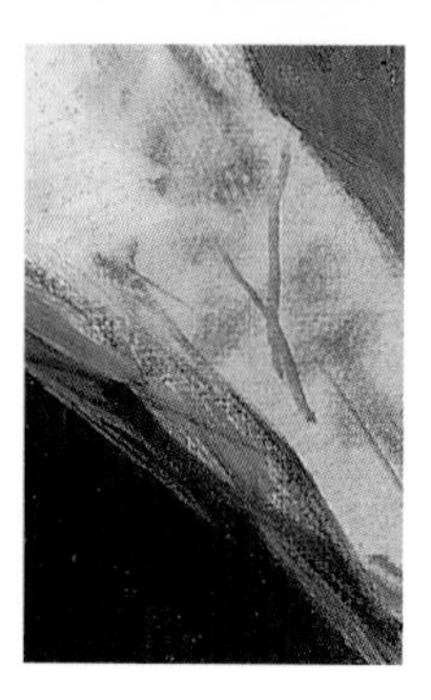

*Women in Gray* was presented in a red frame, while the frame of *Women in a Loge* (p. 75) was bright green. From the critics' perspective, this was her contribution to the overall madness of the exhibitors. The critic, Wolf, wrote that these madmen had once called themselves Impressionists, and although they had now changed their name, their style remained the same. To be criticised along with her new friends, the Impressionists, was a great honour for Cassatt. The weekly satirical magazines *Le Charivari and L'Illustration* had a tradition of publishing caricatures of the most notable paintings as a part of covering the most significant art shows.

Mrs R. S. Cassatt

1889
Oil on canvas, 96.5 x 68.6 cm
Fine Arts Museum of San Francisco,
San Francisco, California

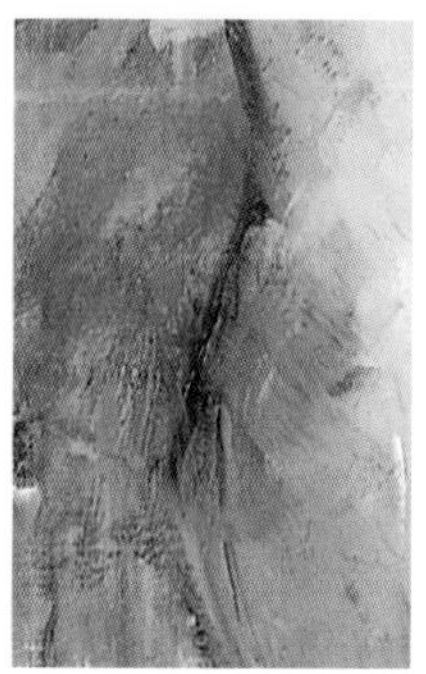

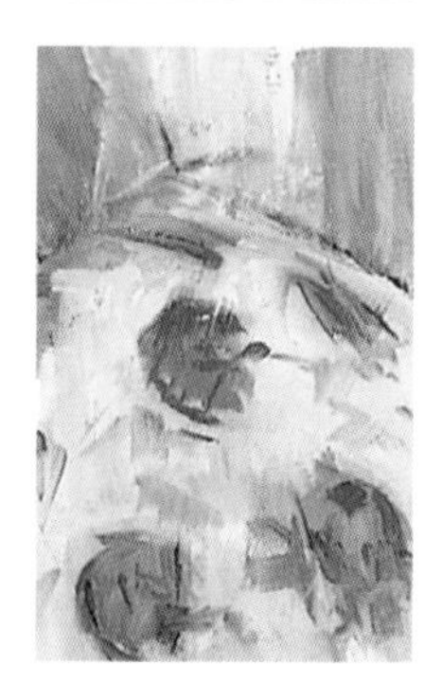

These caricatures were very popular and expressed the public opinion more sharply than critical reviews. On 23rd April 1879, *Le Charivari* published a number of drawings by a popular caricaturist, Jules Renard, under the title *A Day at the "Independents"*. At the centre of the page was a caricature of Mary Cassatt's painting *Women in a Loge* (p. 75) with the caption that read: "Wouldn't she be better off on the balcony?" Cassatt's style provoked mockery due to its democratic nature, while Degas' *Chanteuse de Café (Café-Concert Singer)* was ridiculed as an advertisement for women's gloves. These two pictures were given special attention by the caricaturist and that,

## Emmie and Her Child

1889
Oil on canvas, 90.2 x 63.5 cm
The Roland P. Murdoch Collection,
Witchita Art Museum, Witchita Kansas

Mary Cassatt

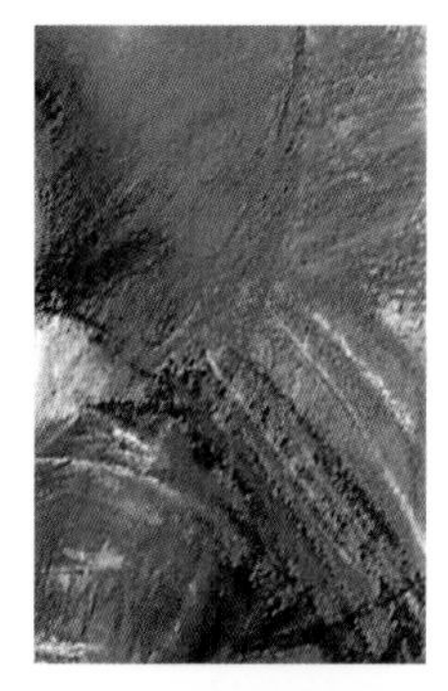

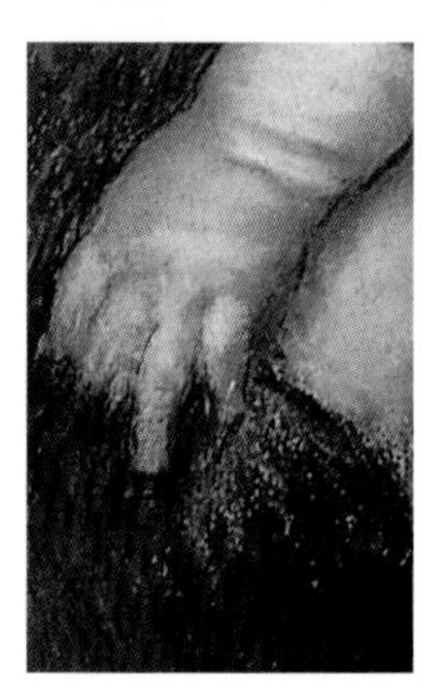

too, was an honour of sorts – taking part in an Impressionist show for the first time, Mary was singled out together with Degas. Since very few pictures were sold at the exhibition, the painters decided to divide the proceeds evenly among the participants. With this money, Mary purchased a painting by Degas and a landscape by Monet. From then on, Mary Cassatt's paintings and drawings became an inseparable part of Impressionist shows, because for the most part they were organised by Degas. In his report on the Fifth Exhibition of 1880 in *Le Voltaire*, the writer, Gustsave Goetschy, related how difficult it had been to find a place to hold it;

Woman with her Child

1889-90
Pastel on tan wove paper, 63.5 x 40.6 cm
William Benton Museum of Art,
University of Connecticut, Connecticut

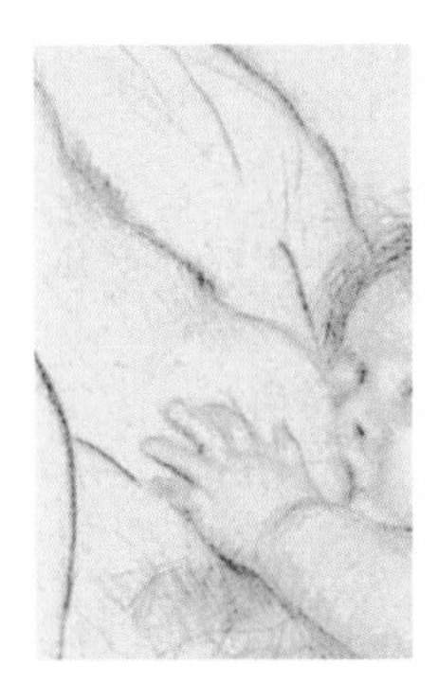

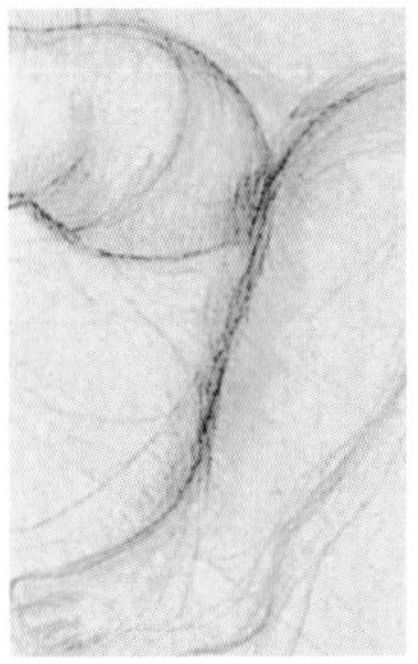

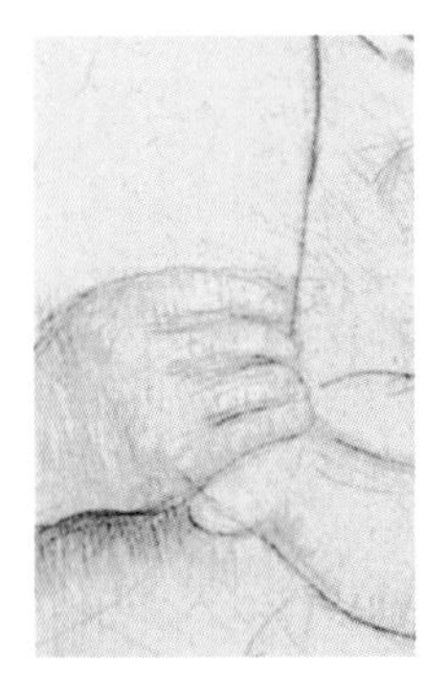

he himself had taken part in the search. Degas would usually start looking for a place as early as February, scrutinising message boards and probing concierges. When the place was finally found, they accepted as many pictures as they could fit in it, and then chose the date for the show. In 1880, they found an apartment in a very good location – on the corner of rue des Pyramides and rue Saint-Honoré, facing the Louvre. That is why, as soon as the show opened – this time on April 1st, exactly a month before the opening of the Salon – it was flooded with visitors, including some famous critics and artists.

The Infant

1890
Drypoint, 23.8 x 17.7 cm
Private Collection

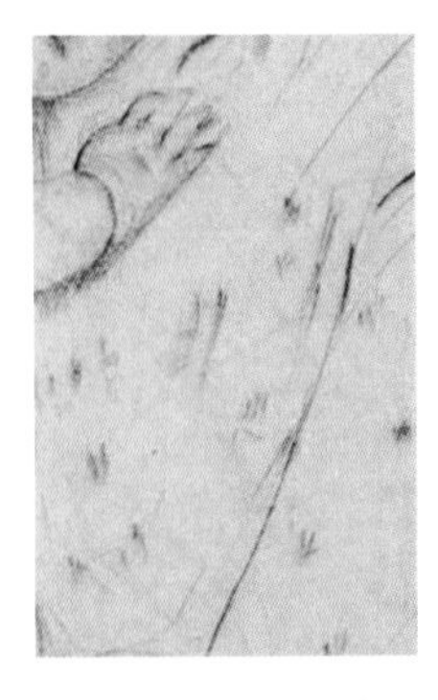

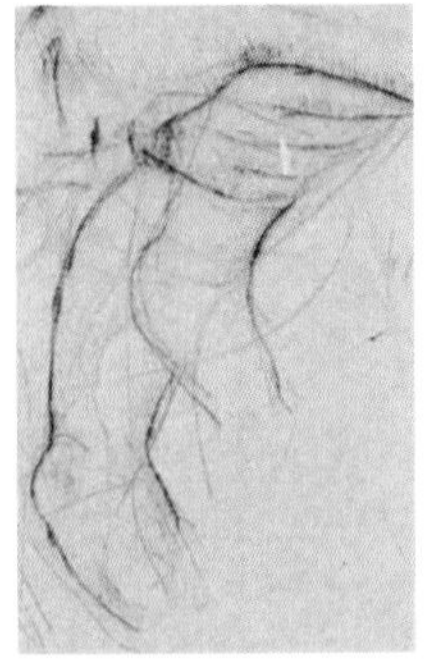

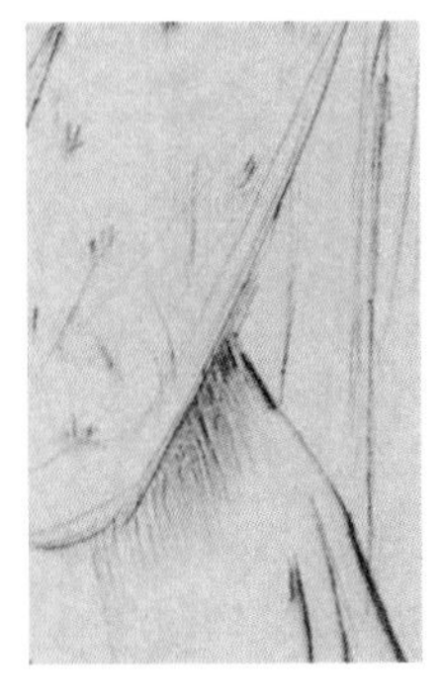

Although construction noise – the building was not finished yet – somewhat disturbed the show's festive atmosphere, it did not discourage visitors. The Fifth Exhibition did not feature paintings by the main Impressionists – Monet, Renoir, and Sisley – but a whole room was reserved for paintings by Degas. In another room hung the works of Berthe Morisot and Mary Cassatt. One would think it unfavourable for paintings by a new participant like Mary Cassatt to be exhibited next to those of an experienced Impressionist such as Morisot. However, the lightness of Morisot's manner only accentuated Cassatt's solid professionalism.

Tranquility

1890
Drypoint, 26 x 17.5 cm
Private Collection

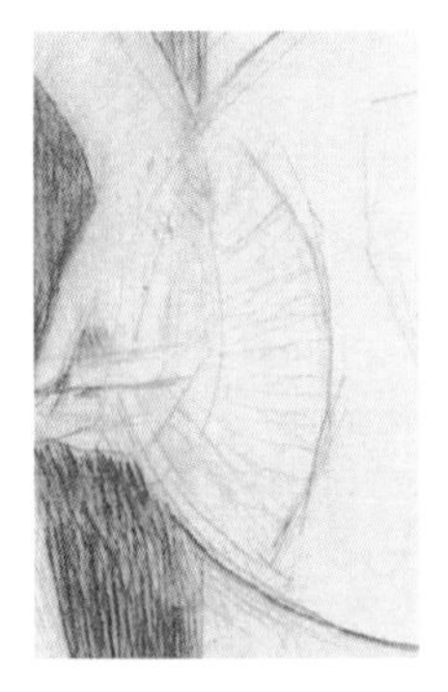

They say that in a conversation in front of paintings by the two artists, Gauguin said: "Miss Cassatt has the same charm, but more force." Mary Cassatt's paintings attracted attention due to the high quality of their execution. The mastery of technique and the informal composition of her paintings and pastels revealed a touch of the influence of Degas, but without mere imitation of her teacher's manner. The critic, Wolf, a persistent detractor of the Impressionists, once again compared the participants in the Fifth Exhibition with madmen, although excluding Degas and Berthe Morisot.

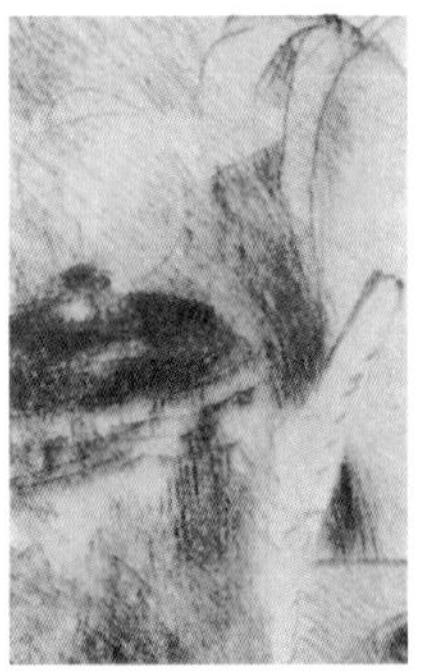

Tea

1890
Drypoint, 17.9 x 15.7 cm
Private Collection

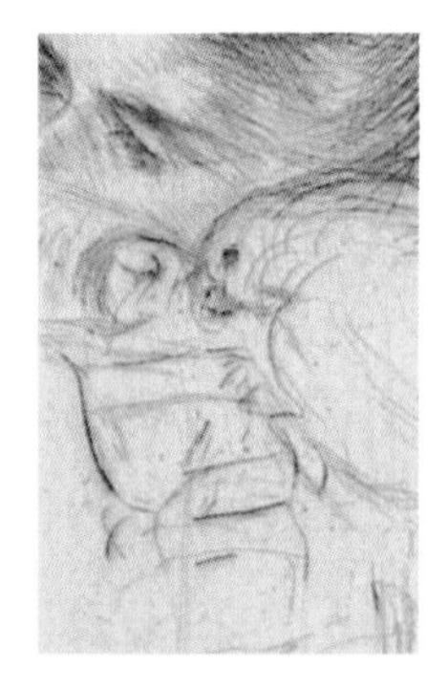

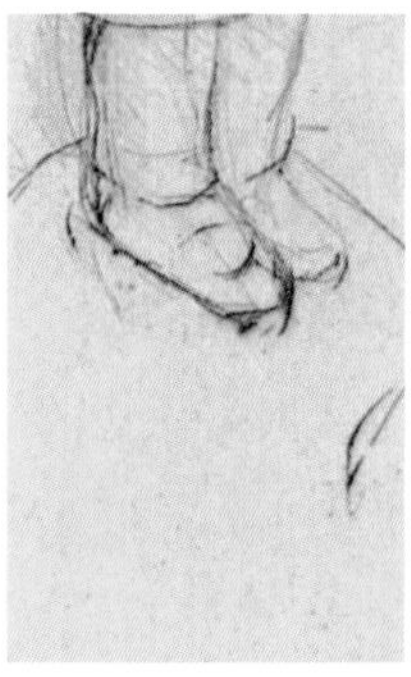

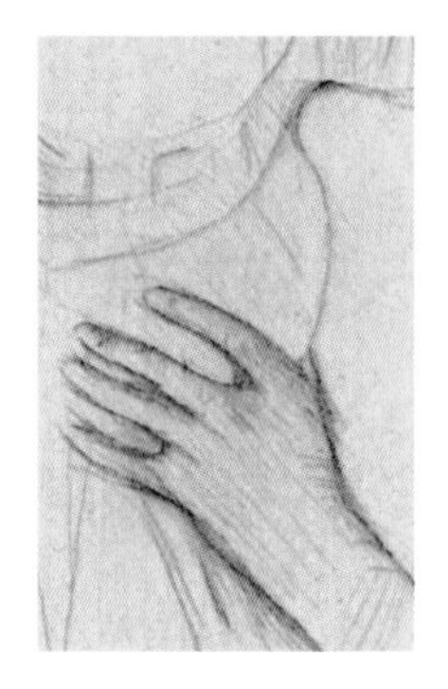

One would like to think that Mary Cassatt, being the student of Degas, was also spared this derogatory title. Henri Mornand referred to impressionism in *La Revue Litteraire et Artistique* as "mad daub". There were, nevertheless, a few critics who supported Impressionist innovation although some of them suspected that the absence of Monet, Renoir and Sisley signified the group's capitulation in the face of conventional art, and the beginning of its disintegration. In his report about the show for *Le Siècle* newspaper, Henry Havard wrote that Impressionism was dying, Monet had gone over to the enemy camp, and Degas was left without students.

The Child and the Parrot

1890
Drypoint, 24 x 16 cm
Private Collection

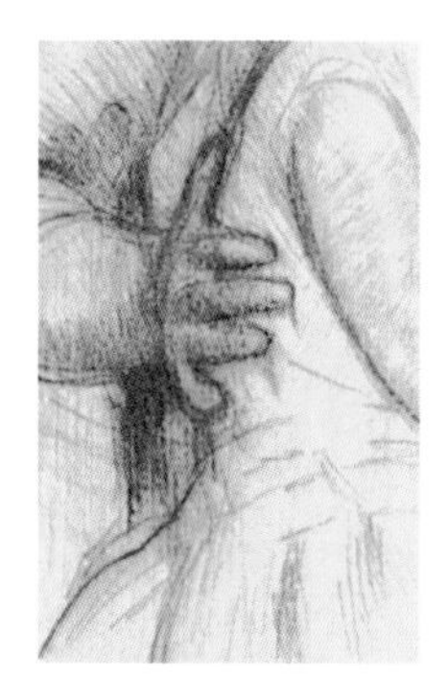

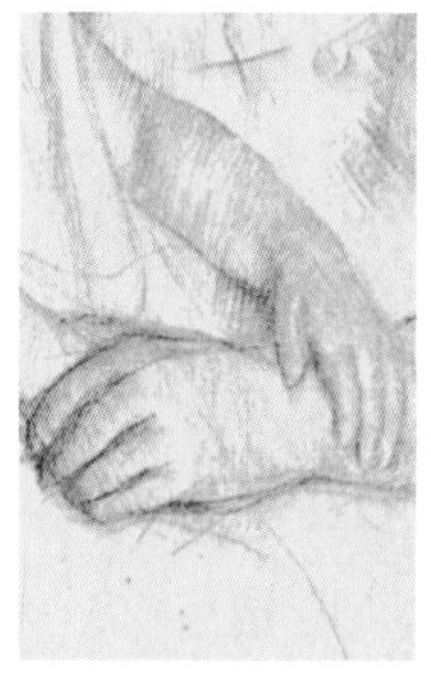

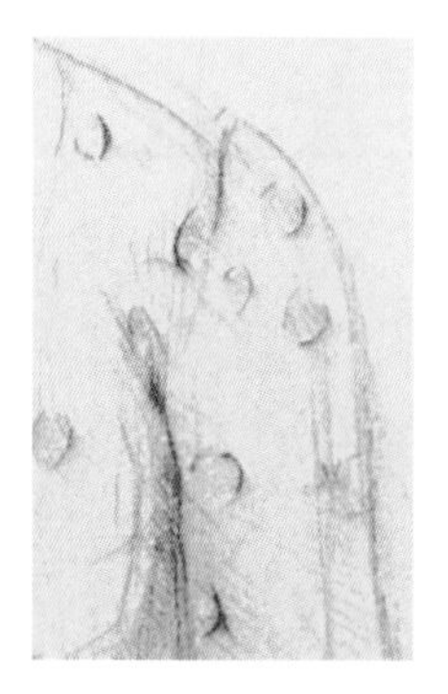

Now Degas had all the more reason to defend the movement with the help of his supporters, among whom Mary Cassatt was practically his only true disciple. Among the critics reviewing the Fifth Exhibition, there was the symbolist writer, Joris-Karl Huysmans, who, in his report in *L'Art Moderne* magazine, gave special attention to all of Degas's protégés. He paid tribute to Raffaelli, who "showed his original individuality in its every expression", mentioned "the invaluable recruitment of the conscientious artist M. Zandomeneghi by the

Rest

1890
Drypoint, 23.6 x 16.8 cm
Private Collection

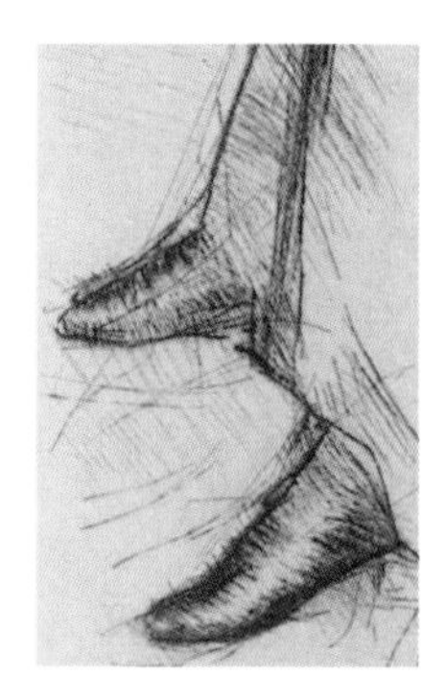

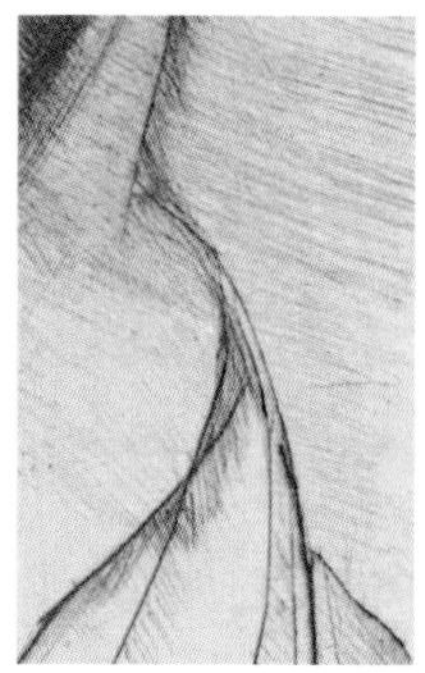

independents," and "another curious painter of certain corners of contemporary life," Forain. His analysis of Mary Cassatt's art was not especially flattering. Huysmans classifies her as a painter of bourgeois society: "Here it is again, the bourgeoisie,... it is a comfortable world, but more refined, more elegant." He believed that the artist's individuality was not yet fully developed. Nevertheless, he recognised her gift: "Mlle Cassatt has, however, a certain curiosity, a special attraction, because the giddiness of feminine nerves shown in her painting is more balanced, more peaceful, more reflective than that of Mlle Morisot."

Reflection

1890
Drypoint, 26.4 x 17.6 cm
Private Collection

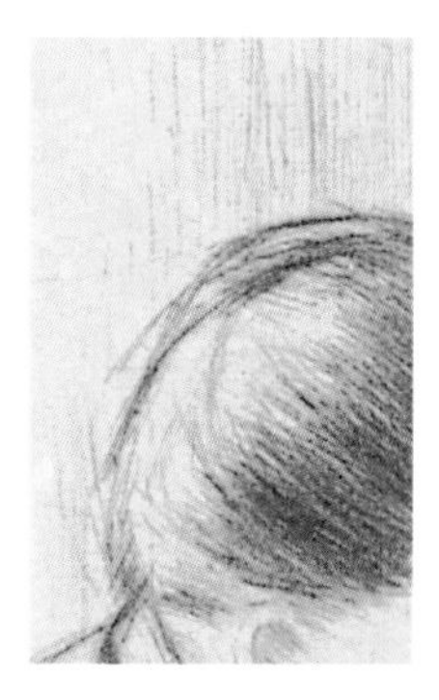

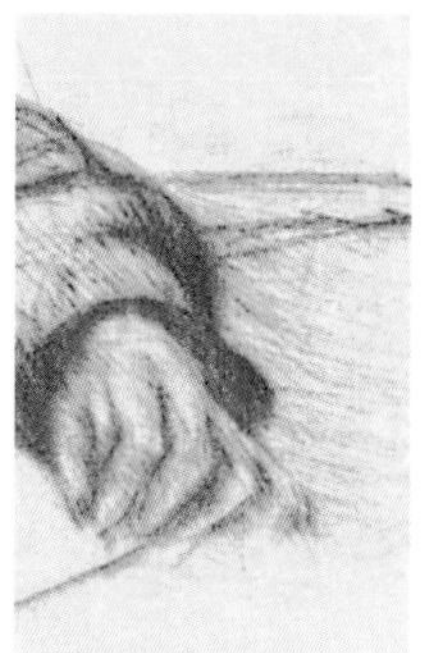

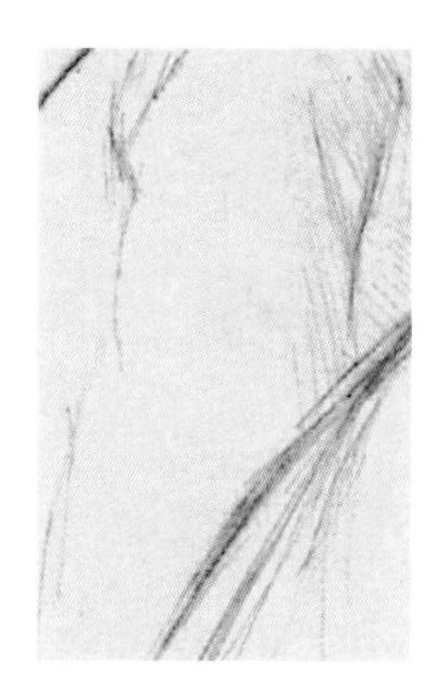

Huysmans analyses influences on her art: "A student of Degas – I saw his influence in that charming picture of a red-haired woman in yellow, examining her back in the mirror on the crimson background of a dressing room – Mlle Cassatt is evidently also a student of English painters..." The Sixth Impressionist Exhibition took place in 1881 at the same address as the First – 35 boulevard des Capucines. Although the only members of the original group were Pissarro and Berthe Morisot, Degas and all of his protégés participated in the show. Mary Cassatt submitted more than ten works,

The Lesson

1890
Drypoint, 16 x 23.4 cm
Private Collection

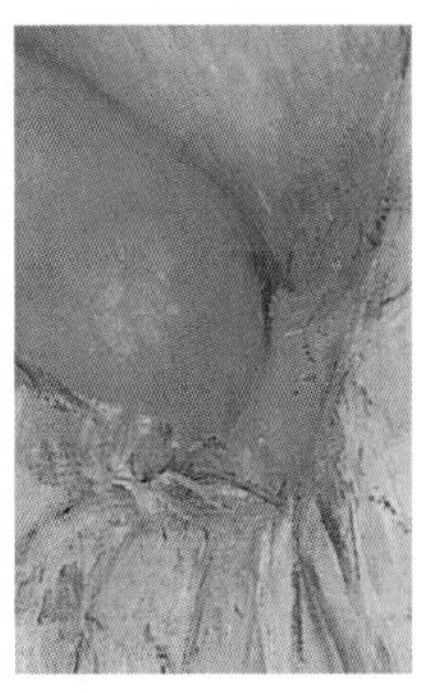

including *Lydia Crocheting in the Garden at Marly (p. 59), Family Group: Mrs. Cassatt Reading to her Grandchildren*, as well as several portraits of women and children. The fairly cautious Huysmans, who at the previous exhibition had pointed out the influence of Degas and the English painters on Mary's work, this time sang her praises. "From these two influences," he wrote, "evolved an artist who now does not owe anything to anyone, an artist entirely her own, entirely unique." Despite her choice of subject, she managed to avoid the pitfalls to which some of the English painters had succumbed: "Mlle Cassatt managed to

## Mother Holding a Child in Her Arms

1890
Oil on canvas, 81.5 x 65.5 cm
Museo de Bellas Artes, Bilbao

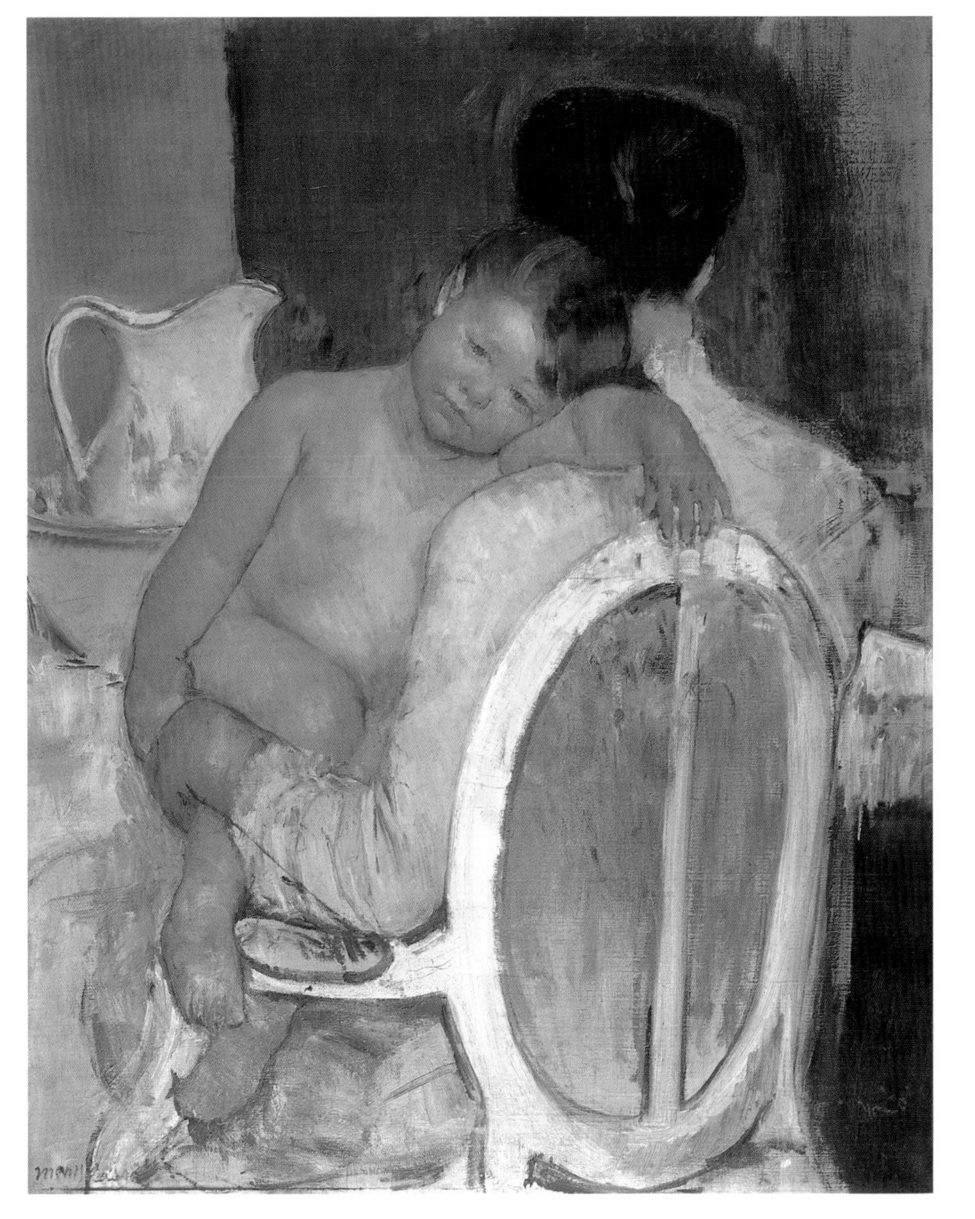

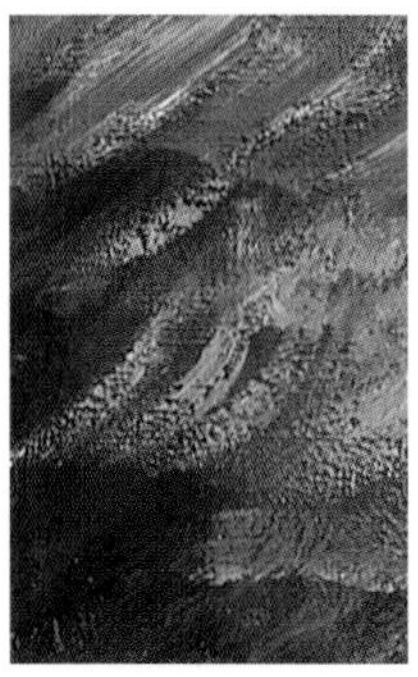

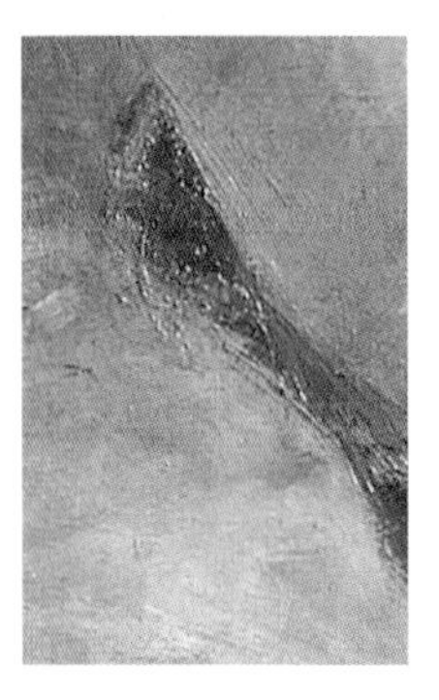

escape the sentimentalism into which most of them fell in all of their works, written and painted". Mlle Cassatt did not belong to those "English and French daubers", those "scribblers" who portrayed children in a frivolous and pretentious manner. "For the first time, thanks to Mlle Cassatt, I have seen delightful pictures of children, quiet scenes from bourgeois life, painted with a kind of delicate tenderness, so charming." Huysmans compares pleasing images painted by Mary with characters from Dickens' novels and concludes: "In this series of works by Mlle Cassatt there is emotive comprehension of a quiet life,

Young Woman Sewing

1890
Oil on canvas, 61 x 48.8 cm
Charles H. S. and Mary F.S. Worcester Collection,
The Art Institute of Chicago, Illinois

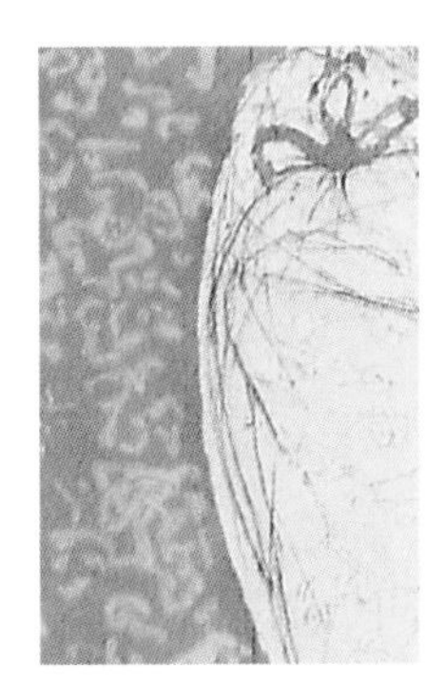

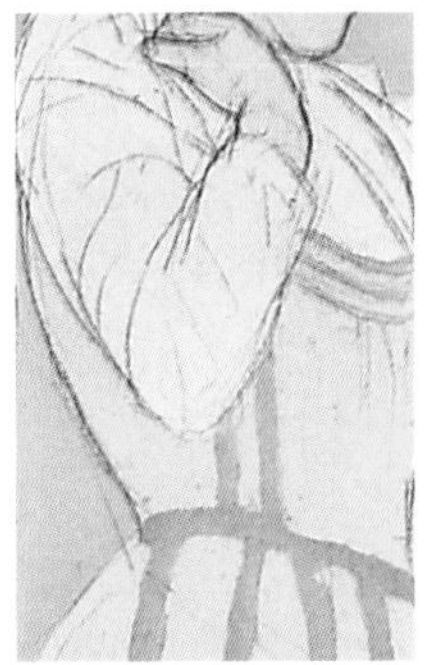

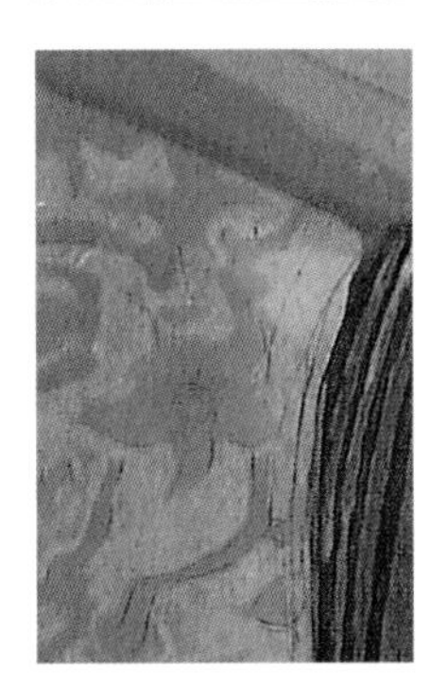

a pervasive feeling of intimacy." The critic does not elaborate on the painter's artistic manner, and for a good reason. For Huysmans, who found it difficult to accept the Impressionists' disorderly dabs, Mary's art represented an acceptable compromise. Solid technique, balanced composition, and almost classical texture of the canvas surface, in combination with fresh, light colours, represented for him a version of impressionism that he was able to accept. The Seventh Exhibition of 1882 did not include any of Mary Cassatt's works. Following Pissarro's request, the organisation of the show was entrusted to the art dealer, Paul Durand-Ruel.

Young Woman Trying on a Dress

1890-91
Drypoint and aquatint on cream laid paper,
95.8 x 65 cm
The Art Institute of Chicago, Illinois

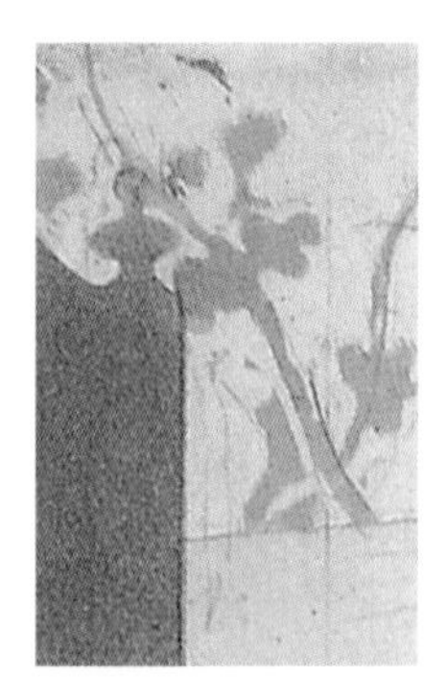

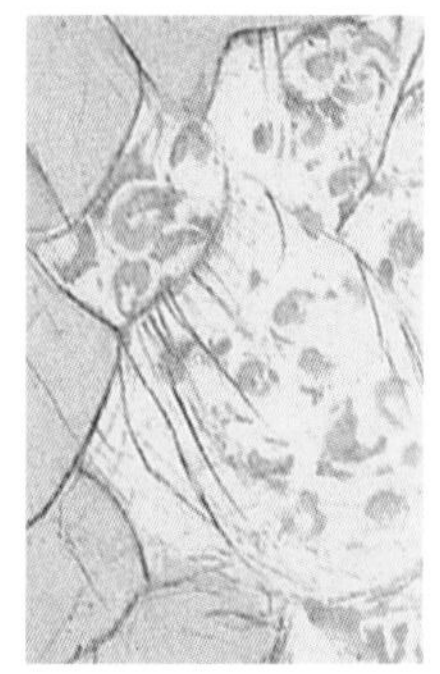

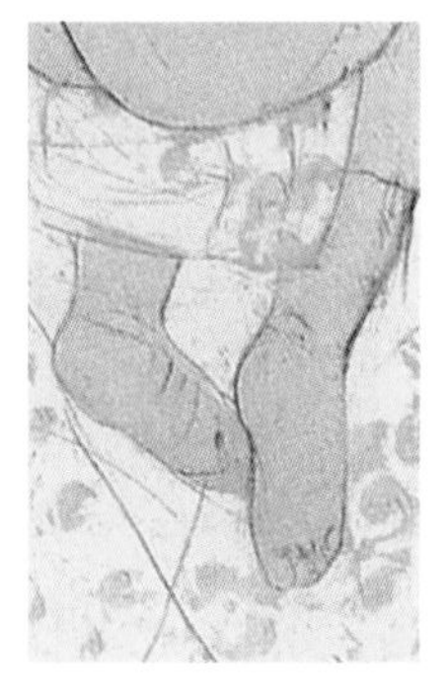

The artists were concerned about discord within the group, which they blamed on the authoritarian character of Degas. The latter withdrew from the show, and so did his *protégés.* Together with Degas, Mary returned to the Eighth, and last, Impressionist Exhibition, which was held at the boulevard des Italiens in 1886, since Degas was once more involved in organising it, in cooperation with Berthe Morisot and her husband, Eugène Manet. Mary's paintings of children were displayed in the same hall with pastels by Degas. In this way, Mary had gone most of the way as the Impressionists although she occupied her own special place within the increasing diversity of the shows.

## Nude Child

1890-91
Drypoint and aquatint on cream laid paper,
36.8 x 26.8 cm
The Art Institute of Chicago, Illinois

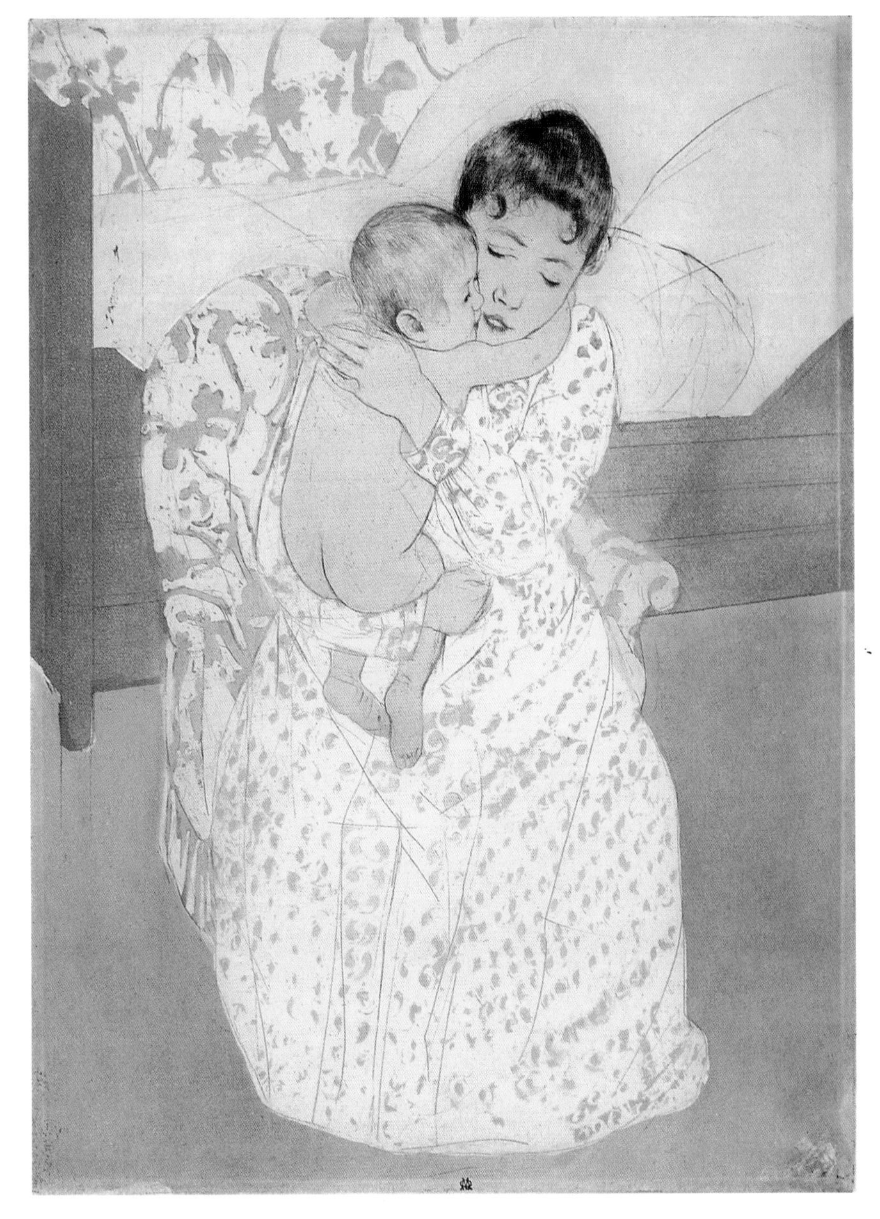

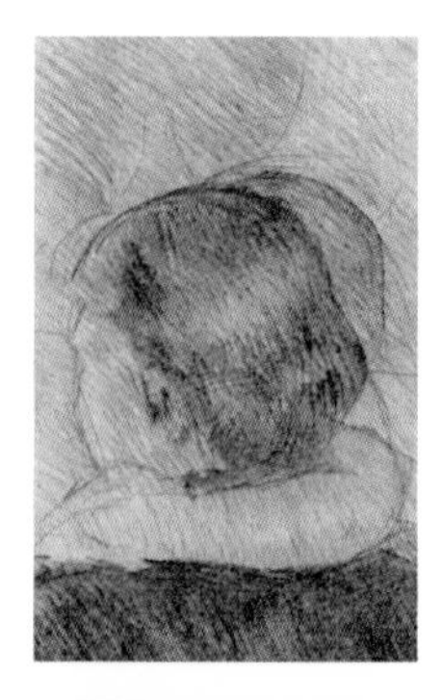

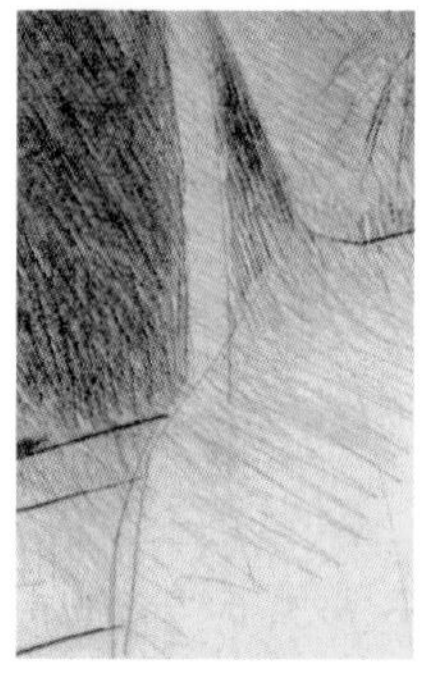

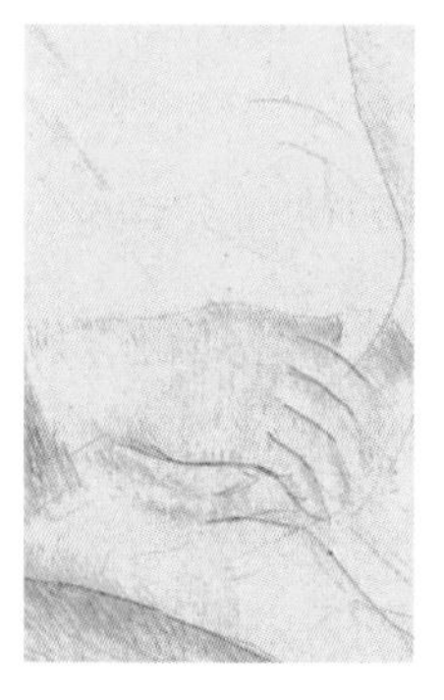

In 1887, the critic, Félix Fénéon, wrote that Degas and Mary Cassatt should be excluded from the ranks of the "luminists" representing pure Impressionism. Nevertheless, "it is true that all of them were searching for a sincere expression of modern life, questioned the usefulness of schooling, and exhibited communally." Fénéon carefully examined the strengths and weaknesses of Mary's work: "Mlle Mary Cassatt, an American, a student of M. Degas, represents children and young girls, solid studies done in a distinguished and knowledgeable manner, although in somewhat harsh colours and in a dispassionate manner."

The Mirror

1891
Drypoint, 22.8 x 17 cm
Private Collection

Critics unanimously refer to Mary as the student of Degas. She did not try to hide her admiration for everything he created. "She recognised and admired Degas as one of the greatest classic masters of French art," wrote Ségard. "And she understood very well that patient and persistent study of his less famous masterpieces was an opportunity for enrichment." Degas' idea of artistic education, with his admiration for old masters, resonated with Mary. "You need to copy and re-copy the masters," said Degas, "and it is not until you have proved yourself as a good copier that one can reasonably let you copy a radish from nature."

The Parrot

1891
Drypoint, 16.2 x 12 cm
Private Collection

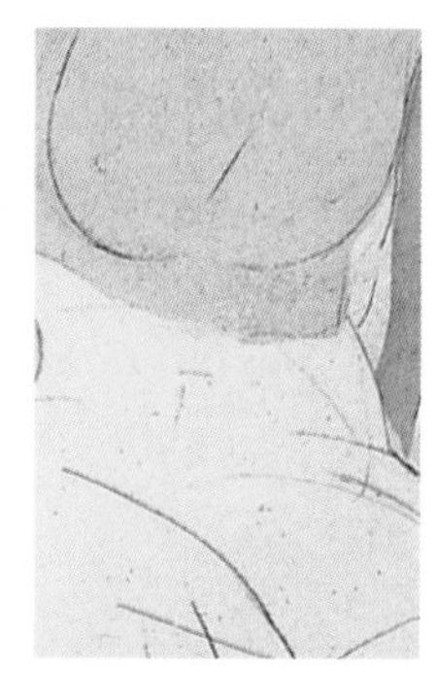

Mary herself walked in the shoes of a copyist. Contemporaries insist that Mary was never an actual student of Degas. However, his opinion about her works was always very important to her. Even in 1891-1892, when she was working on a decorative panel in Chicago, her customers turned specifically to Degas for evaluation. Everyone knew very well that Degas could be sharp and caustic in his criticism, and Mary appreciated his praise all the more throughout her whole life.

The Coiffure

1890-91
Drypoint and aquatint on cream laid paper, 36.5 x 26.7 cm
The Art Institute of Chicago, Illinois

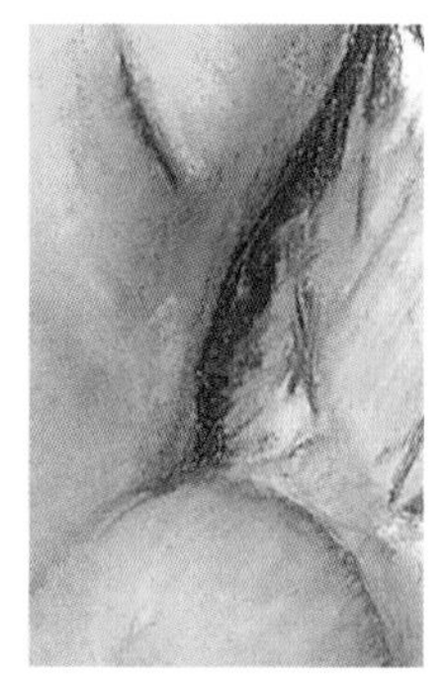

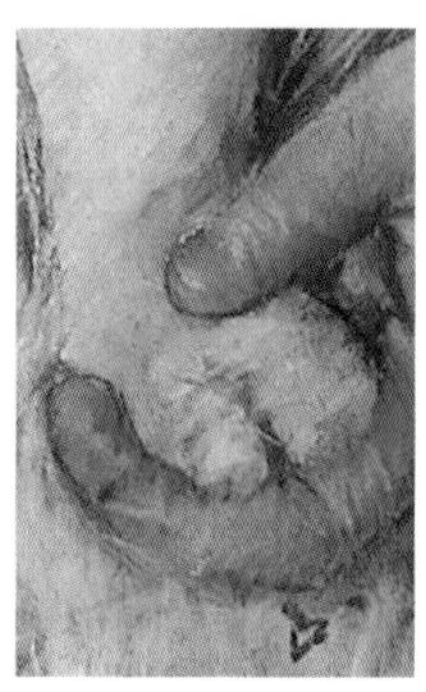

"I am very happy that M. Degas liked the most recent pictures; he is sometimes too kind." she wrote in 1905. Degas did indeed sincerely admire Mary Cassatt's work and considered her to be his equal. They say that Degas once whispered in front of her picture: "I cannot admit that a woman can paint as good as this." Vollard mentioned many times that Degas considered Mary very talented. He wanted to own her work, and at the 1886 show, Degas offered his best "nude"–*Femme au bain (Woman in Tub)* – in exchange for Mary's study of a girl combing her hair.

Baby's First Caress

1891
Pastel on paper, 76.2 x 61 cm
Harriet Russell Stanley Fund, New Britain Museum of American Art, New Britain, Connecticut

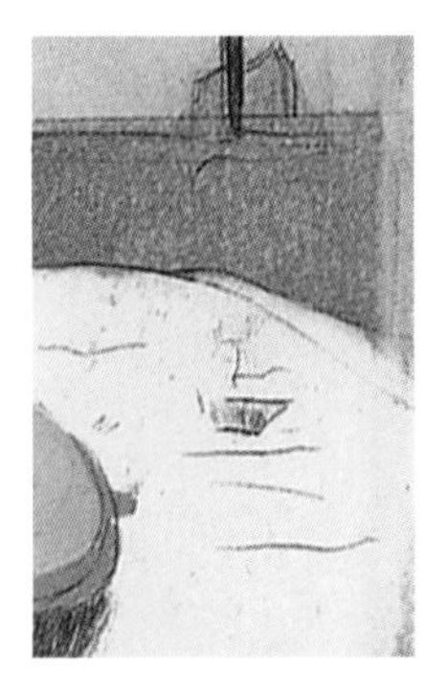

It is possible that Degas was also attracted to Mary because of her learning – she read a great deal, was a friend of Mallarmé, and was interested in history and archaeology. Mary Cassatt's biographer, Achille Ségard, claims that "there was nothing sentimental in the sympathy which drew Miss Mary Cassatt to this group of outcasts." Degas' role in Cassatt's artistic biography is so great, however, that it is not surprising that researchers ask the question: "Was there more than just friendship between Mary Cassatt and Degas?" Degas was so secretive that even his closest friends knew very little about his private life.

In the Omnibus

1891
Drypoint and aquatint on cream laid paper,
38.4 x 26.7 cm
The Art Institute of Chicago, Illinois

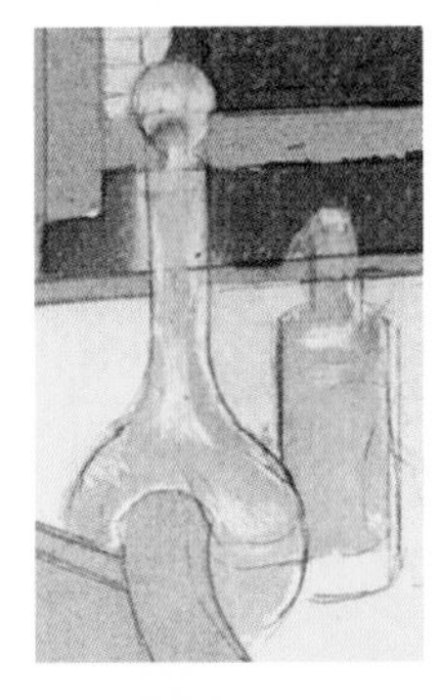

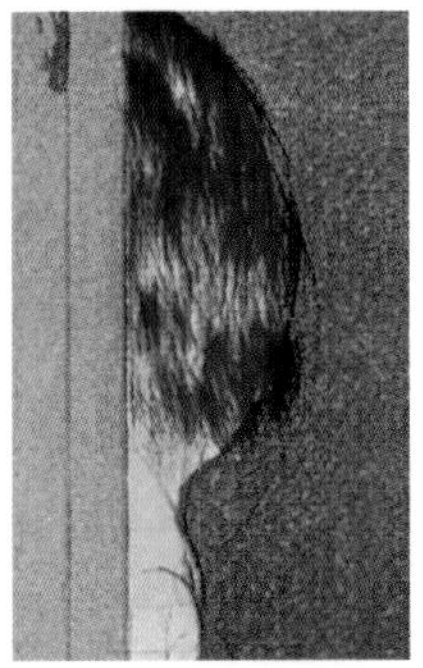

And although most biographers believe that he and Mary were connected by friendship alone, this friendship was fairly tender and intimate. Mary's name appears over and over in Degas' emotionally reserved letters. "My dear Pissarro, I congratulate you on your ardour," Degas wrote in 1880, having received some engravings by Pissarro, since, at the time, they both shared a passion for etching. "I ran to Mlle Cassatt with your package. She offers you the same compliments as I." Degas always respected Mary's opinion and highly valued her work. "Mlle Cassatt makes wonderful attempts at etching," he wrote to Pissarro.

Woman Bathing

1891
Colourprint with drypoint and aquatint,
36.4 x 26.8 cm
The National Gallery of Art, Washington D.C.

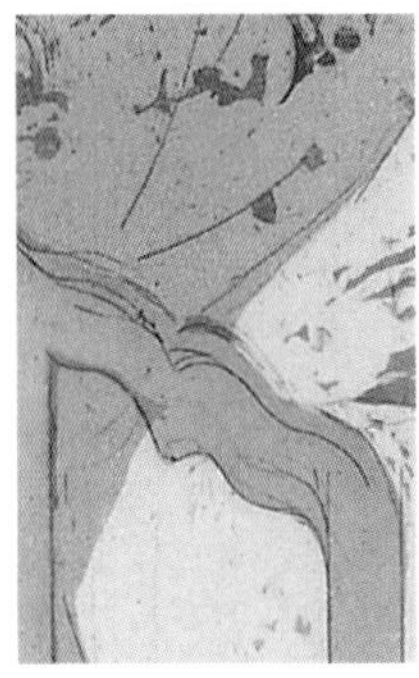

Sometimes his references to Mary appear quite intimate. Having learned of the death of a sister of one of his friends, he writes "...after what Mlle Cassatt told me this morning..." And then, quite uncharacteristically for Degas, there is a romantic recollection: "Do you remember that evening of guitar playing at home, almost a year and a half ago?... Mlle Cassatt should have come..." In 1880, Degas informed his friend Henri Rouart about Mary's return to Paris with her sister and parents: "The Cassatts returned from Marly." That year, for the first time, Mary's brother, Alexander Cassatt, visited Paris with his family.

Afternoon Tea Party

1891
Colourprint with drypoint and aquatint,
33 x 25.4 cm
The National Gallery of Art, Washington D.C.

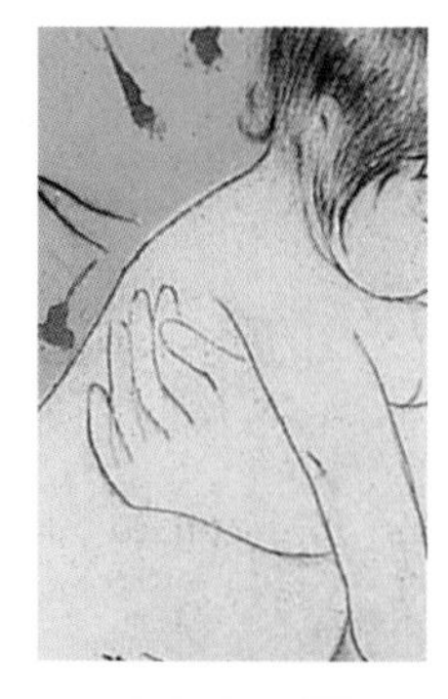

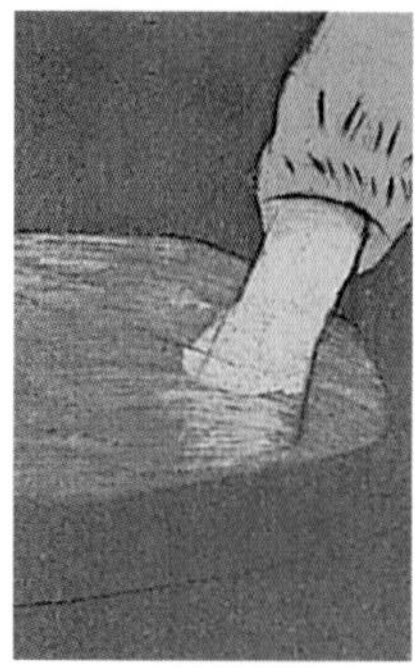

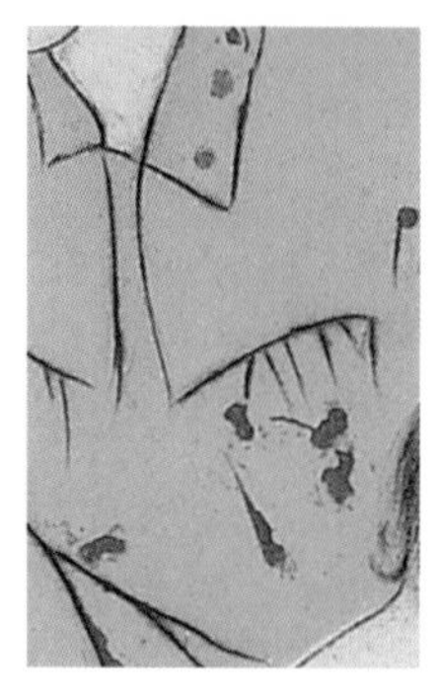

Mary and her relatives spent most summers in the suburbs west of Paris where the Impressionists enjoyed working and where their landscape was born for the first time – in Marly-le-Roi and Louveciennes. One summer, in Oise, she happened to be neighbours with Pissarro. Mary was never arrogant and took advantage of every opportunity to learn. She said that that summer she and Pissarro often worked outdoors together. "Pissarro," says Miss Cassatt, "was the kind of teacher who could teach rocks how to draw properly!"

The Bath

1891
Drypoint and aquatint on cream laid paper,
32.1 x 24.7 cm
The Art Institute of Chicago, Illinois.

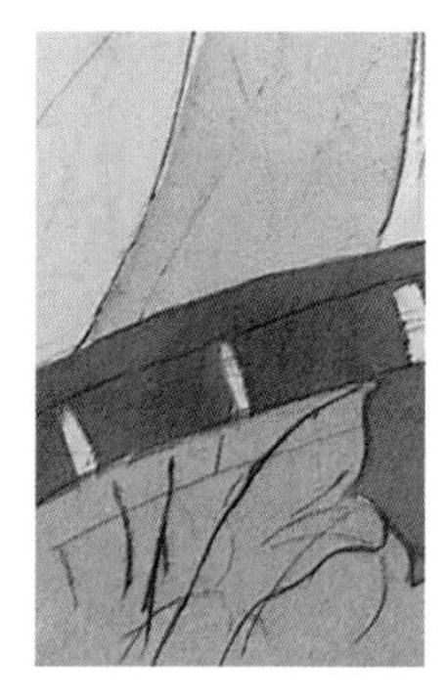

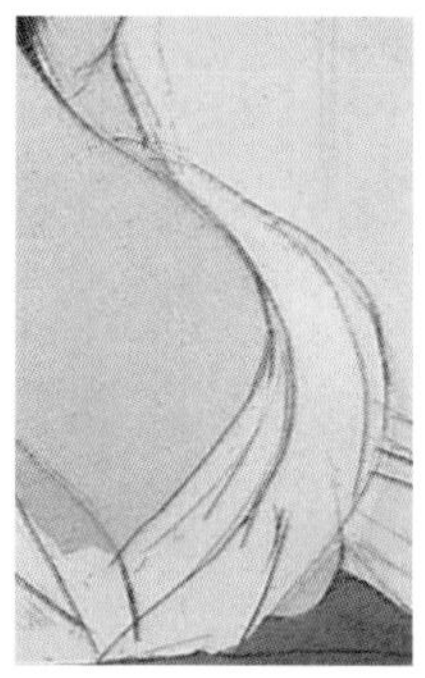

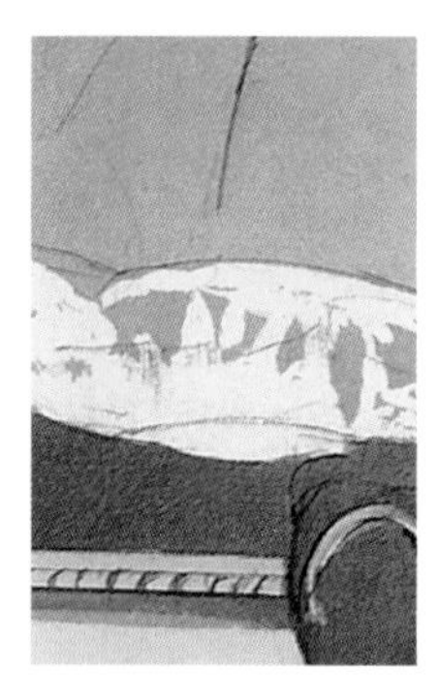

Nevertheless, those sessions did not play any significant role in her career, since she almost never painted landscapes. Mary was very attached to Paris; she adored the city and could not bear to be away from it for a long time. Even after she later settled on the Oise, she constantly returned from there to her Paris apartment. In Paris, she was attracted to the Impressionists' favourite spots. She lived on rue Trudaine, near Montmarte; her studio was located at 6 boulevard de Clichy. Possibly it is this studio that is mentioned in one of the letters by Degas: "Mlle Cassatt took a studio on the ground floor which did not seem reasonable to me."

The Lamp

1891

Drypoint and aquatint on cream laid paper,
32.3 x 25.2 cm
The Art Institute of Chicago, Illinois

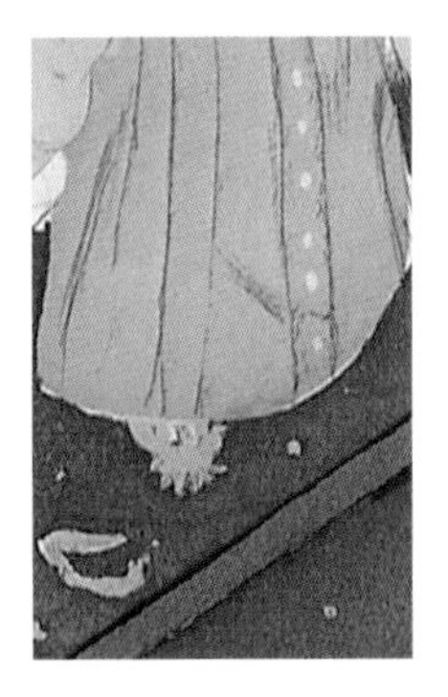

In 1884, she moved near the Champs-Élysées, to rue Pierre Charron, and, later, in 1887, moved permanently to 10 Rue Marignan, where she had an apartment and a studio. A letter by Degas, as usual, contains compliments addressed to Mary: "That which she was doing in the country, she continues to do very well in the studio. It is much more solid and noble than what she did last year." When Degas began writing sonnets, he dedicated one of them – "Perroquets" – to Mary Cassatt. It seems that among the photographs taken by Degas himself, there were also pictures of Cassatt.

The Letter

1890-91
Colour print with drypoint and aquatint,
34.5 x 21.1 cm
The Art Institute of Chicago, Illinois

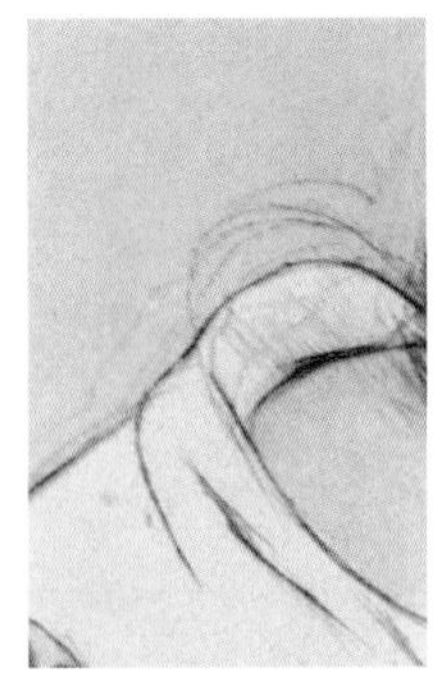

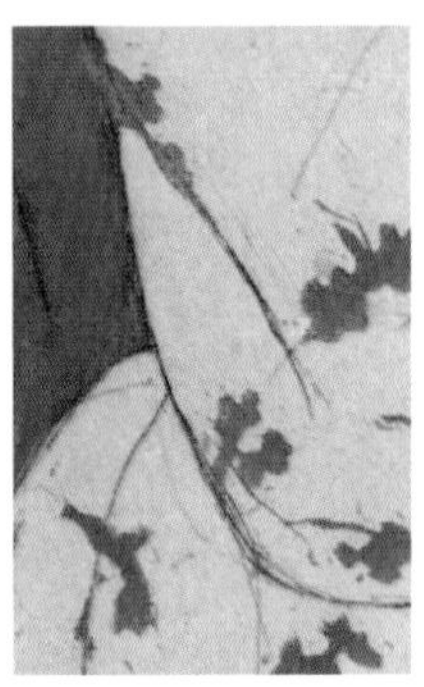

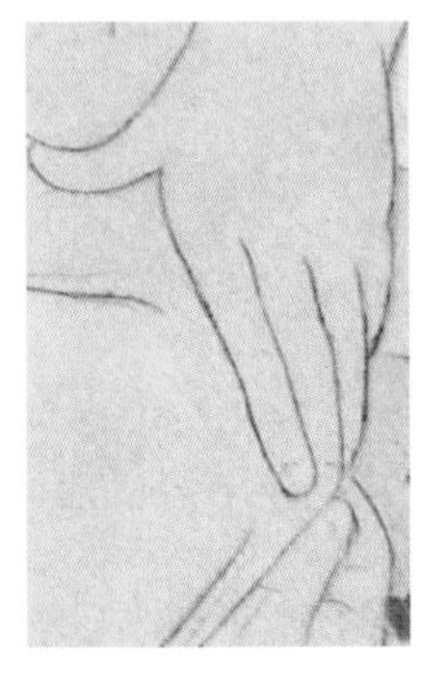

The most vivid evidence of Degas's interest in Mary Cassatt, however, are his drawings, prints, and pastels. He drew Mary's portrait many times, some of which were later made into prints: *Mary Cassatt au Louvre, (Mary Cassatt at The Louvre).* Sometimes Mary is trying on a fashionable hat *(Chez la Modiste) (At the Milliner's),* sometimes she is sitting on a chair with playing cards in her hands – *Miss Cassatt, Seated, Holding Cards.* Mary must have especially liked this portrait, since she wanted to buy it.

Mother's Kiss

1891
Colour print with drypoint and aquatint,
37.2 x 27.6 cm
Rosenwald collection, The National Gallery of Art,
Washington D.C.

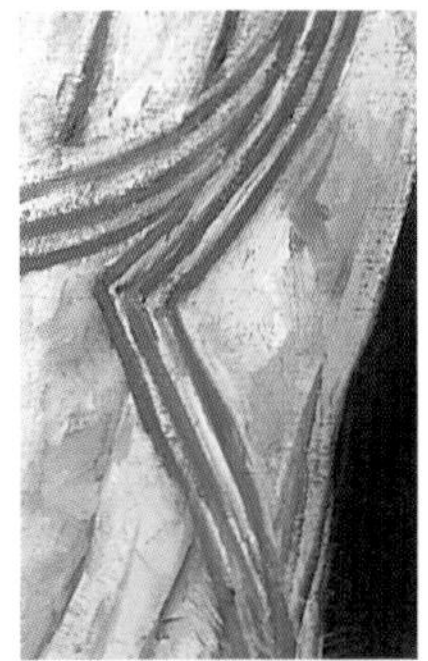

She always admired the work of Degas, but towards the end of her life she saw features in his portraits of her that almost scared her. In 1912, she wrote: "It is the portrait that Degas painted of me, hanging in a room next to the salon (my studio), which I would especially like to get rid of... I especially don't want to leave it to my family as my portrait. It has qualities of a work of art, but it is so sad and represents me as a person so repugnant that I do not want anybody to know that I posed for it."

Woman with a Red Zinnia

1891
Oil on canvas, 73.3 x 60.3 cm
The National Gallery of Art, Washington D.C.

Mary Cassatt

However, Mary's slender figure and narrow face are easily recognised among the cast of Parisian characters depicted by Degas in the course of his life. Mary gradually, but naturally, entered the circle of Impressionists. Berthe Marisot wrote many letters to her sisters, mother, and her close friend Stéphane Mallarmé. She had a gift for telling stories with sincerity and ease, and her letters communicate the atmosphere of the Impressionist circle and of dinners in her own family.

Young Woman picking Fruit

1891
Oil on canvas, 52 x 36 cm
Museum of Art, Carnegie Institute,
Pittsburgh, Pennsylvania

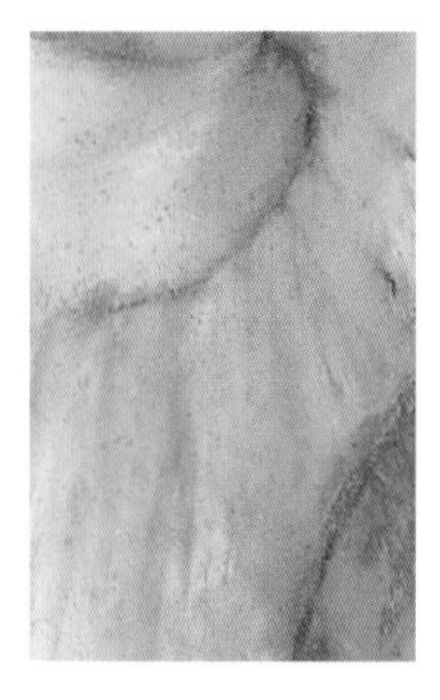

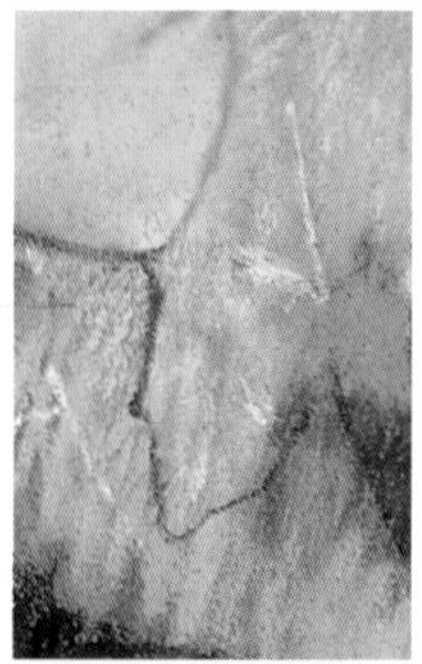

Berthe describes the shows and meetings with friends, and Mary Cassatt's name often appears in her letters. In August 1883, she wrote to her brother Tiburce: "If you talk to Mlle Cassatt, she will probably be of use to you, ... she is very intelligent." From the first show where they exhibited together, there was a sincere sympathy between these two female painters. Berthe respected Mary and held her in high regard.

Contemplation

1891-92
Pastel on tan wove paper, 66 x 51 cm
Private Collection.

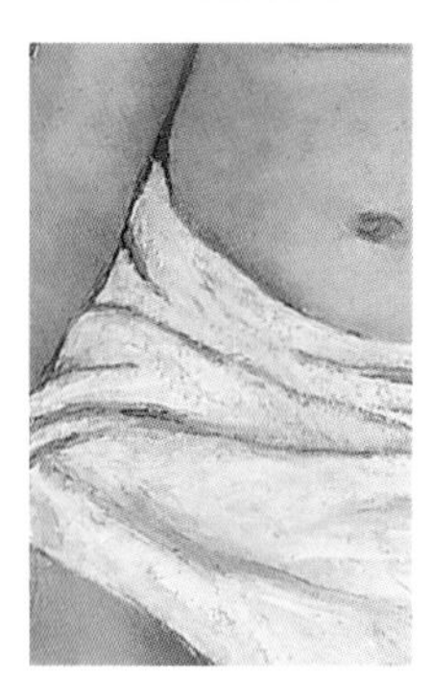

When Mary was absent from friends' gatherings for a long time, Berthe began to worry: "Have you seen Miss Cassatt lately?" In the fall of 1888, in his letter inviting Berthe to Valvins, Mallarmé writes: "It is September, dear lady, and the sun shines less and less. Are you still up to spending a week in the country?... Miss Cassatt seemed to be counting on you very much and I encourage it." Mary became an inseparable member of their circle. At the beginning of the twentieth century, as the friends of her youth passed away one by one, Mary often suffered from loneliness.

The Bath

1892
Oil on canvas, 99.1 x 66 cm
The Art Institute of Chicago, Illinois

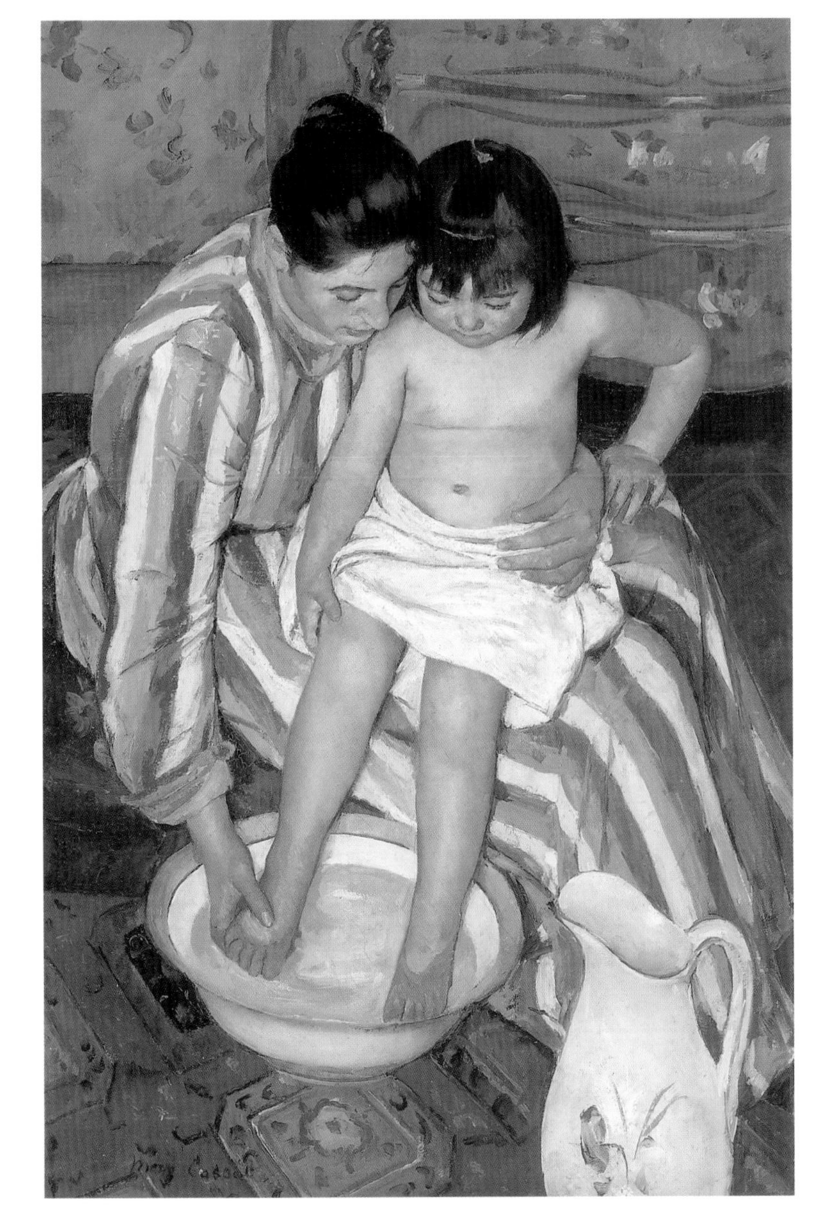

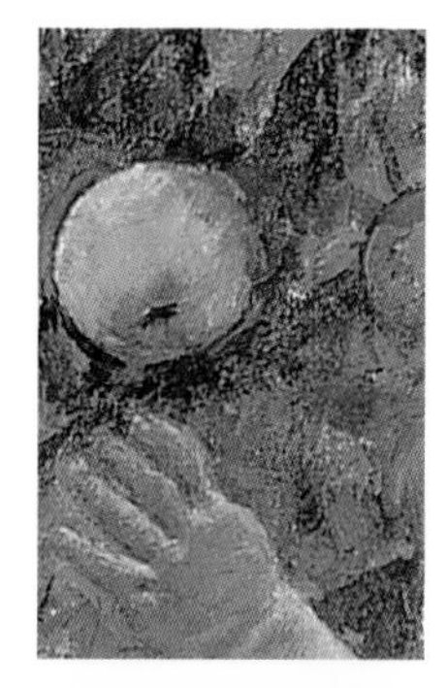

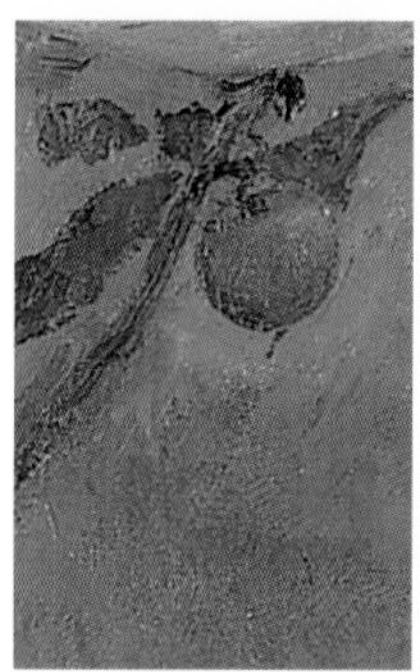

The state of her health forced her to live in the South, in Grasse, from where she wrote to Durand-Ruel, their art dealer: "I don't work anymore, I am bored here all alone..." Not far from her, in his villa in Cagnes, lived Renoir. Severe arthritis completely deprived him of the ability to move. He could not rise from his chair and his fingers could no longer hold a brush. "It was really painful for me to see poor Renoir in that state," Mary wrote after visiting him, "If only I could do something for him! In my opinion, he is poorly cared for."

## Child Picking a Fruit

1893
Oil on canvas, 100 x 65 cm
Virginia Museum of Fine Arts, Richmond, Virginia

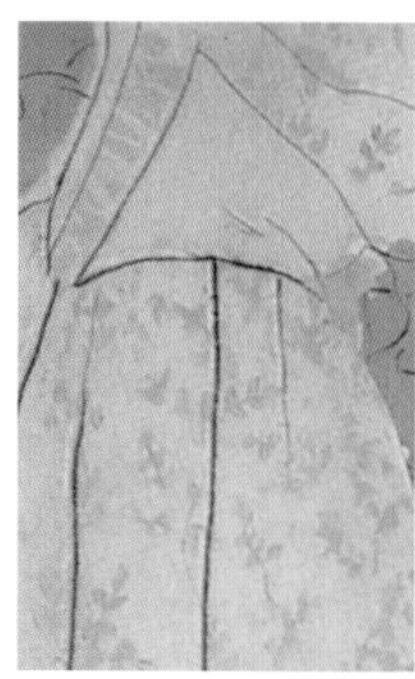

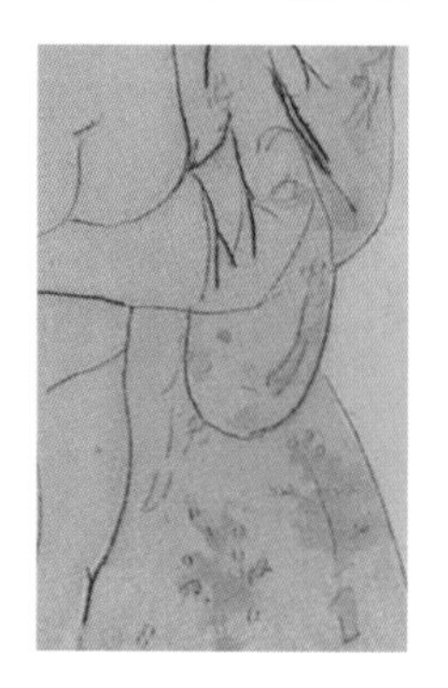

When Renoir met young Aline Charigot in Montmartre, Berthe Morisot said with jealousy that a plain seamstress was a poor match for an artist. Mary's comment must have echoed these past conversations. Nevertheless, Aline Renoir became Renoir's faithful friend and walked the difficult journey of his life with him until the end. Together with other friends, Aline searched for doctors that could help Renoir, and Mary followed the results of this search with concern. "They have just discovered a remedy for his illness, but too late for him to be cured by it," she wrote with bitterness in 1913.

The Kitchen Garden

1893
Drypoint, softground etching and aquatint on paper,
42.2 x 29.8 cm
National Gallery of Art, Washington D.C.

Friendships were strong among the Impressionists, and the misfortune of one was shared by everyone. This is why Mary was so disturbed by the news that the story of Renoir's poor condition might reach the newspapers. She was worried about an artist who had visited Renoir, and "who described him as having a brush attached to his hand, and so on, and so forth. What do you think about this? And then Blanche is going to write an article in *Le Gaulois* giving a sad description of the state of Renoir's health." The courage with which Renoir struggled against incurable disease and continued to work inspired her respect and pride.

In the Garden

1893
Pastel over black oiled paper,
on tan wove paper, 73 x 60 cm
Baltimore Museum of Art, Cone Collection,
Baltimore, Maryland

Mary Cassatt

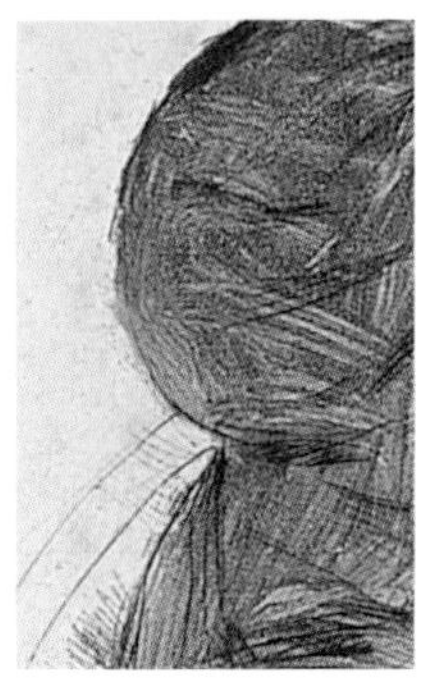

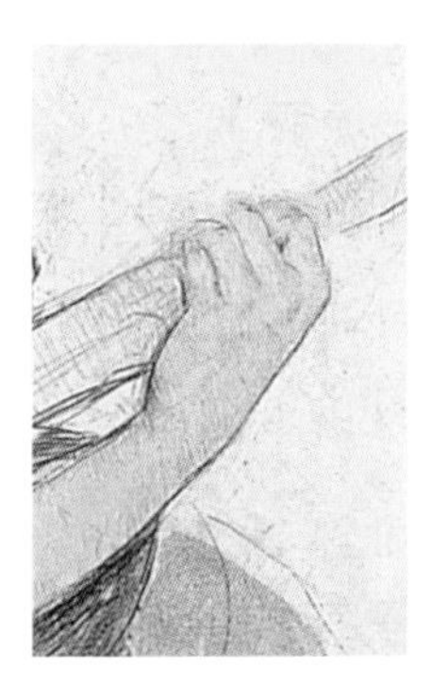

"I have seen M. Renoir, who seemed to be doing quite well," she wrote in 1914. "The great statue is making progress." Paintings by the old Impressionist still impressed her. "I saw Renoir this afternoon," she wrote in 1915, "doing very well, sharp and with a lovely colour in his face, less pale." What did Mary have in common with her contemporaries in art and what set her apart? Mostly, she knew how to learn. In her early works, the influence of the old masters whom she observed in European museums, is obvious.

The Banjo lesson

1893
Drypoint and aquatint in colour, 29.7 x 23.8 cm
The National Gallery of Art, Washington, D.C.

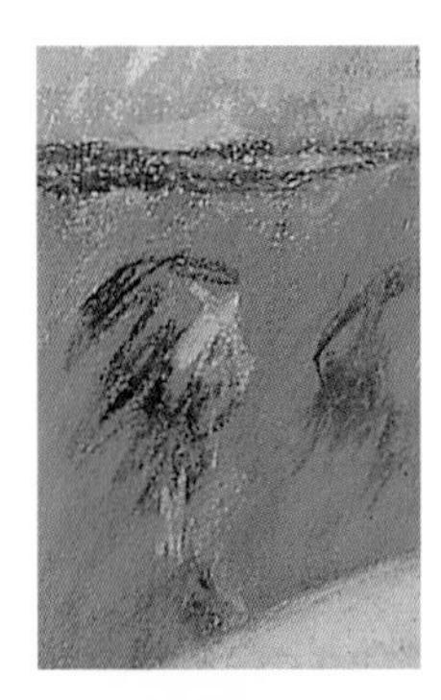

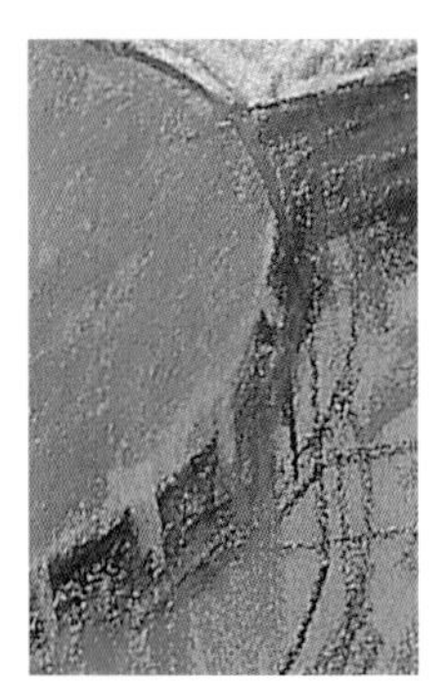

Her admiration for Spanish painters is evident in everything, beginning with the very subject of her paintings – playing the mandolin, balcony, torero. The choice of her own genre – portraits of women and children – was probably influenced by numerous representations of the Madonna by Raphael and his contemporaries. No wonder she spent so much time in Rome. The light effects in her painting testify to her deep admiration of Caravaggio. An 1877 portrait, *Miss Mary Ellison* (p. 65), dating from her stay in Holland, points to her admiration of Vermeer. From this great Dutch master she learned how to create a harmony of colours using cold, scattered light.

## The Banjo Lesson

1893-94
Pastel over oiled pastel
on tan wove paper, 72.2 x 58.6 cm
Virginia Museum of Fine Arts, Richmond, Virginia

Mary Cassatt

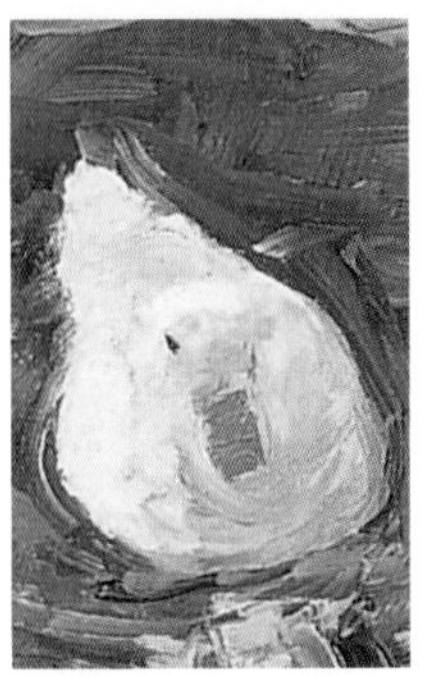

In his art, she was able to discern what was often hidden from many others: a special human warmth, perhaps resonating with her own perception of life. The blue and golden hues in the portrait of *Miss Mary Ellison* (p. 65) recall the subtle colours of Vermeer's *The Lacemaker,* in the Louvre. In the darkened eyes and slightly raised corners of the girl's mouth, one can read a combination of shyness and dignity. Mary's passionate fascination with Rubens, beginning in the Prado, her quest to see everything ever created by the Flemish master,

Summertime

1894
Oil on canvas, 100.7 x 81.3 cm
Terra Foundation for the Arts;
Daniel J. Terra Collection, Chicago, Illinois

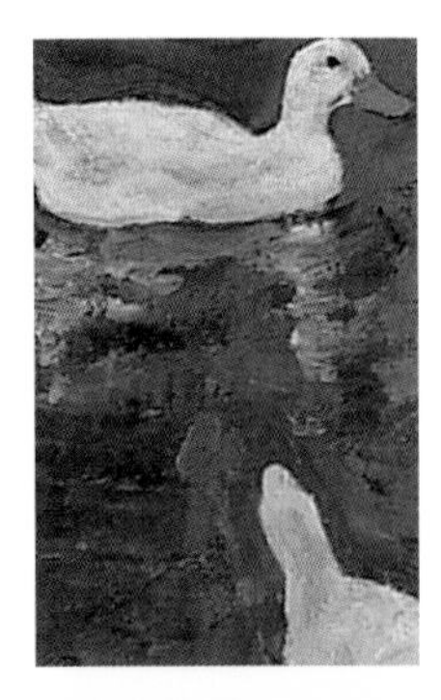

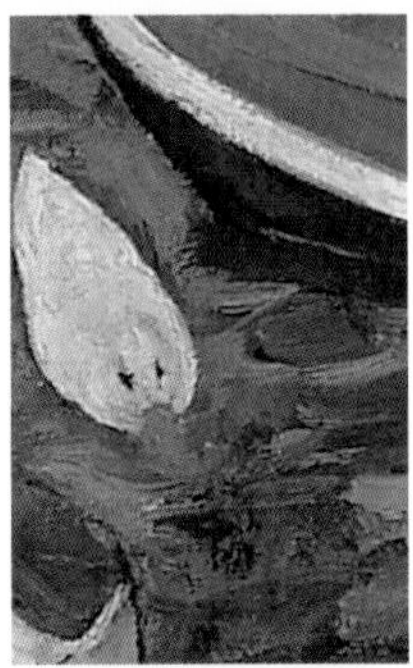

her journey to see the work of Rubens in Belgium – all of these demonstrate the firmness of her resolution to immerse herself in the artistic legacy of the classics. When talking specifically about the influence of Rubens on the painting of Mary Cassatt, one is reminded most of all of his portrait, *Helene Fourment and Her Children*, in the Louvre. The intimacy of this picture, in contrast with the usual lavishness of his paintings, was perhaps one of the landmarks in her search for her own style. In addition, one should not ignore the impression made on her by the English masters.

Summertime

1894
Oil on canvas, 73.6 x 96.5 cm
Armand Hammer Collection,
Los Angeles, California

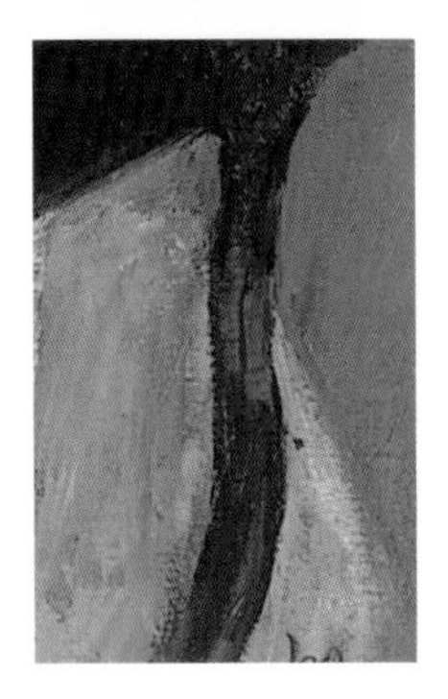

It is not surprising that Huysmans mentioned them in connection with Cassatt's art. An echo of the women's and children's portraits by Reynolds is found in Cassatt's works at all stages of her career. The analytical examination of classical art was the course of study that Mary, who possessed to a rare degree both practicality and diligence, created for herself and followed. The true character of Mary's work was fully apparent from the moment she joined the group of Impressionists. In 1879 she created a whole suite of paintings devoted to a woman in a theatre box.

In the Park

1894
Oil on canvas, 75 x 95.2 cm
Collection of Mr Fayez Sarofim

Mary Cassatt immediately joined the world of Impressionist art, about whose paintings the critic Philippe Burty said in 1875: "They are like small fragments of a mirror of universal life, and swift and colourful things, subtle and charming reflected in it deserve attention and celebration." Some of Mary's paintings are very similar to Renoir's compositions – not to *In The Box* which was presented at the First Exhibition in 1874, but rather to *The Café-Concert*. In Mary Cassatt's picture *At the Opera*, the composition and the woman's pose completely replicate Renoir's painting.

The Boating Party

1894
Oil on canvas, 90 x 117.3 cm
The National Gallery of Art, Washington D.C.

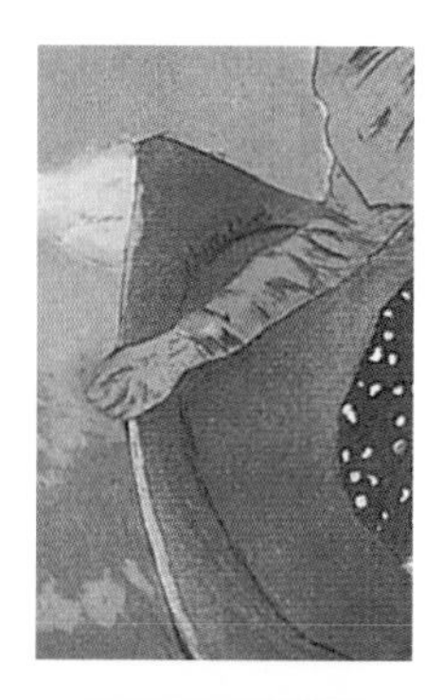

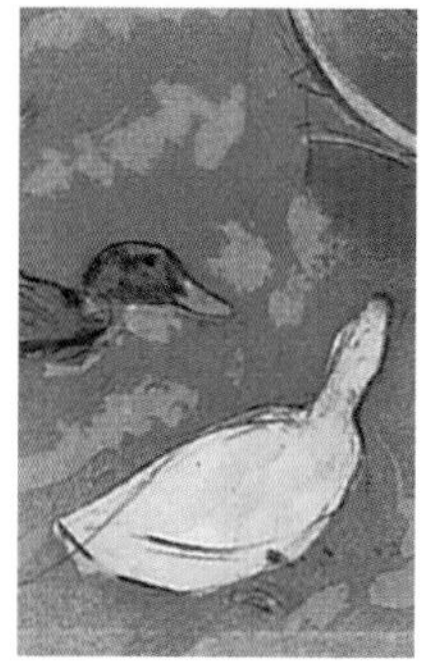

However, this similarity is only external. Mary proceeds instead in the manner of Degas: the suite of her theatre scenes reflects the world of the theatre hall as the ballet scenes of Degas reflect the world behind the curtain. With characteristic sensitivity, Mary understood right away what Burty was writing about: "M. Degas – will he not be a classic when his hour comes? No one will be able to better communicate the sense of modern elegance with a more confident hand." Contemporary high society, especially Parisian society, was Degas' signature theme, and Mary Cassatt found her subjects in the same milieu.

Feeding the Ducks

1895
Drypoint with monotype additions
on cream laid paper, 29.5 x 39.3 cm
The Art Institute of Chicago, Illinois

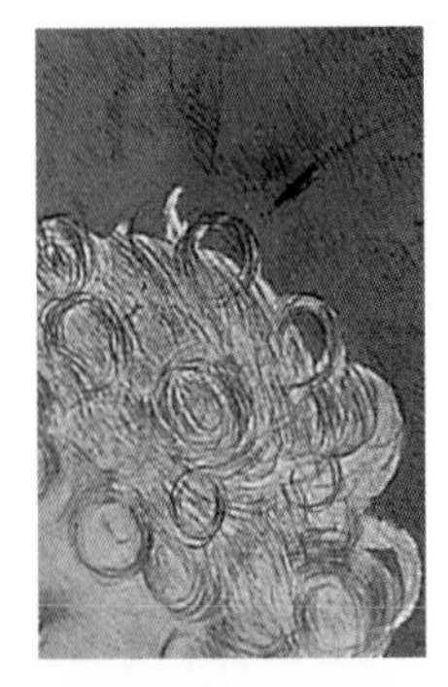

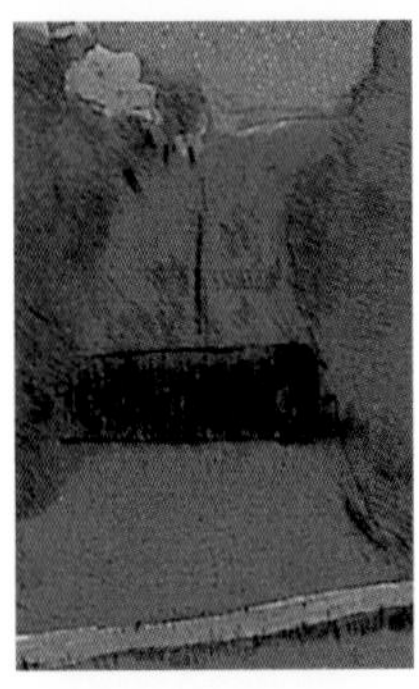

There were different ways to bring them to the audience. The fashionable scenes painted by Degas' friends, Nittis and James Tissot, whose works hung in London and New York museums, had the most success among art lovers. They had an engaging subject, elegance, and an abundance of precisely presented details of costume and interior design. Mary chose a different way; the features of Impressionism pointed out by Armand Sivestre appealed to her: "...above all, it is harmonious. What distinguishes it is therefore the simplicity of its means of harmony. Indeed, one soon discovers that its whole secret is in a very fine and precise observation of the relations between colours."

Young Mother in a Park in front of a Pond

1896
Drypoint and aquatint in colour, 33 x 42.9 cm
Private Collection

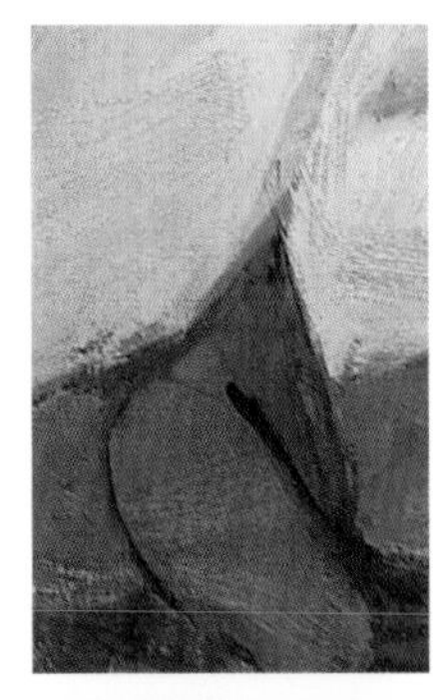

In the work of Degas, Mary found a new language of expression which reflected contemporary life. She was attracted to the mastery of his technique and the precision and beauty of his lines, which were not typical of other Impressionists. Mary painted women adjusting their hats and scarves and putting on gloves, communicating a naturalness of movement that can only be achieved through deep and precise observation. The experience of Degas taught her how to observe and remember and then to draw from memory. She trained her eye in the same way the Impressionists did. She managed to capture on canvas the instant when a mother touched her child,

Ellen Mary Cassatt in a White Coat

1896
Oil on canvas, 81.2 x 60.3 cm
Boston Museum of Fine Arts, Boston, Massachusetts

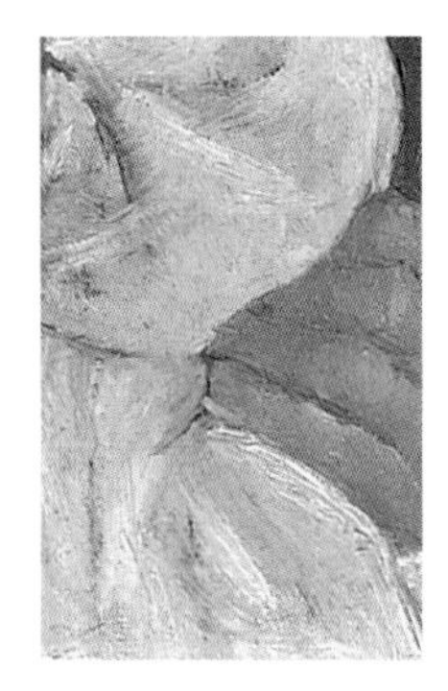

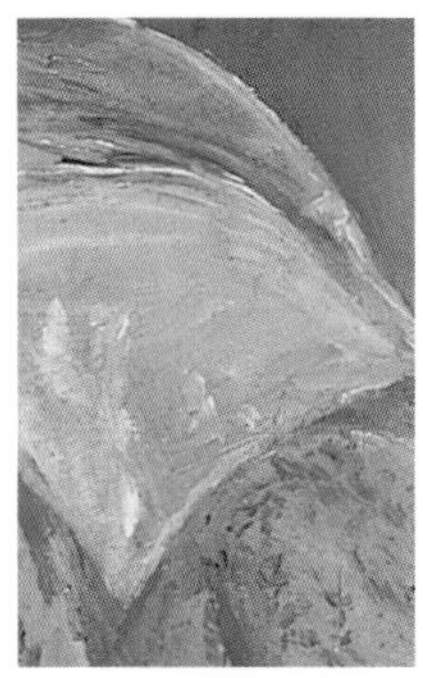

as well as the gesture of an infant who cannot be forced to pose. Mary, however, did not possess the cold objectivity of Degas, for whom observation was a goal in itself and who could not be distracted from it by any emotion. In her works, Mary frequently displayed a purely feminine sensitivity that neither Degas nor Renoir possessed. One could imagine that Mary's always beautiful, always urbane, models were not appealing to Degas. According to Ségard, however, Mary once did find a model in the style of Degas: "She chose for a model a very ugly woman, a servant of a vulgar sort. Mary made her pose in a nightdress at her toilette table,

Maternal Caress

1896
Oil on canvas, 38 x 54 cm
Philadelphia Museum of Art, Philadelphia, Pennsylvania

Mary Cassatt

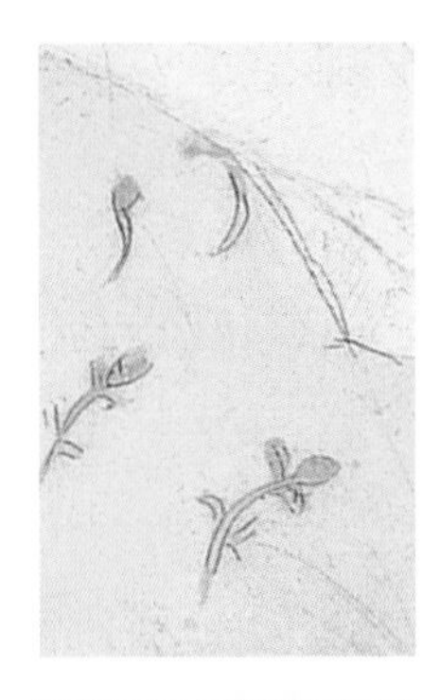

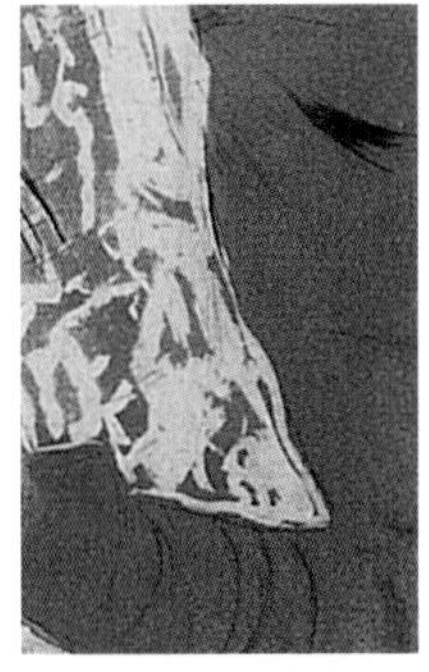

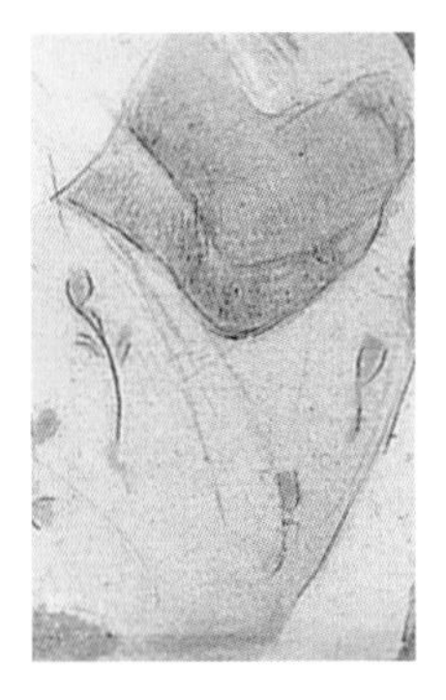

with the appearance of a woman who is getting ready for bed, with her left hand reaching down her neck for a thin tress which has escaped from her hair, and with the other hand pulling this tress to tie it back up… When Degas saw the picture he wrote to Miss Cassatt: "What a picture! What style!" It should be said to Mary's credit that, in representing women and children in her numerous canvasses, she did not follow the example of her teacher, Chaplin, in producing sentimental, saccharine art. Her magnificent technique, mastery of composition, and soft, light palette not only bring her close to her Impressionist friends,

Child with Bare Feet

1896-97
Drypoint and aquatint in colour, 23.5 x 30.8 cm
Private Collection

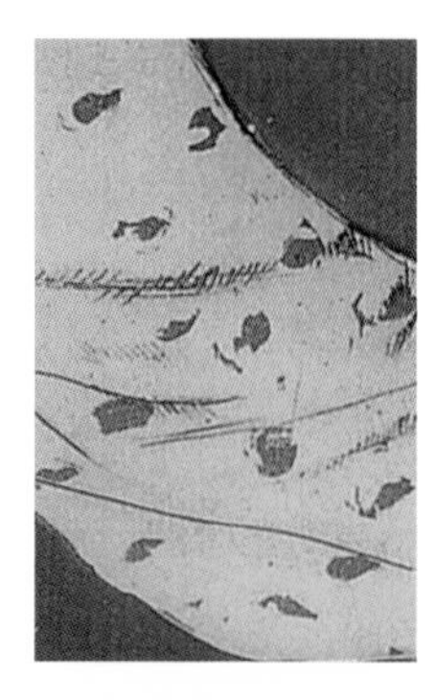

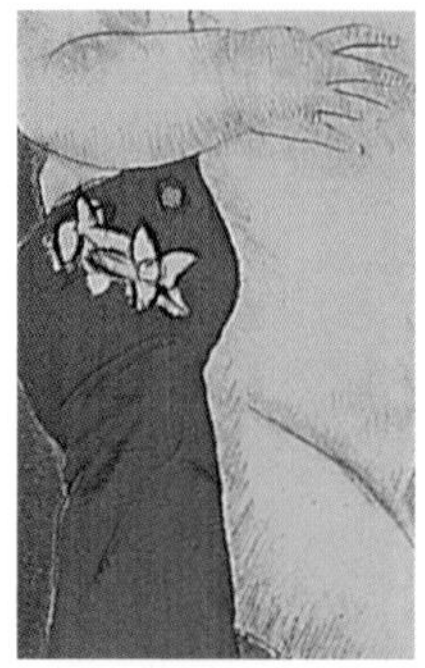

but also make it possible for her work to be considered Impressionist art, and not simply as "women's art." Her friends and family members often served her as models. Even when working on a portrait, however, she almost always considered it a painting – her sister, Lydia, or her friends read, sew, play with children, or sit in a theatre box. She only rarely focused more deeply on the character of the model herself. Her portraits simply communicate the living charm of modern women and children. In the realm of portrait painting, she essentially did the same as Renoir. Her contemporaries considered her portrait of the printmaker,

On the Grass

1897

Drypoint and aquatint in colour, 40.6 x 28.7 cm

Private Collection

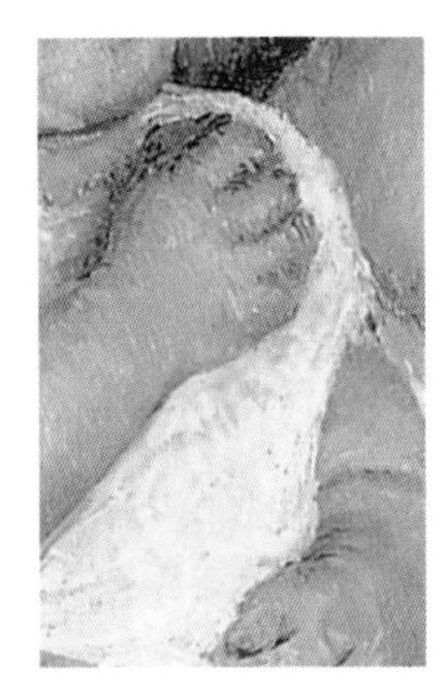

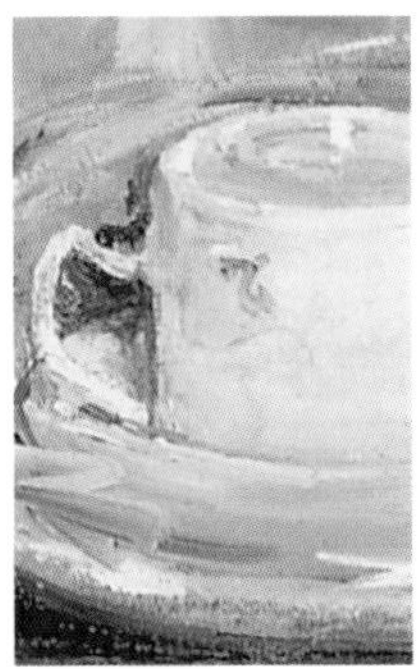

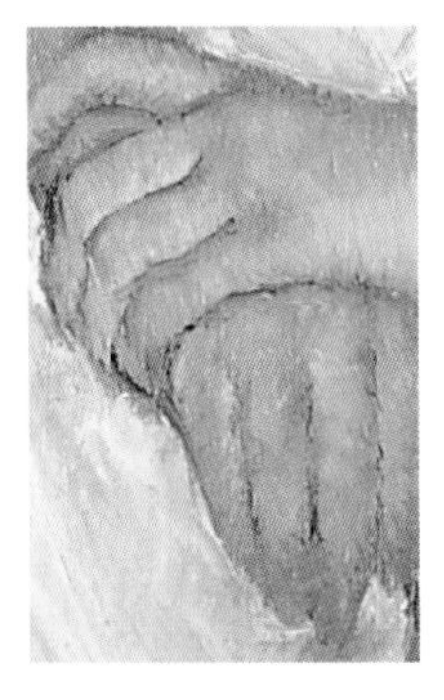

Marcellin Desboutin, to be among Mary's best works. Ségard writes that "Miss Mary Cassatt also painted a portrait of Degas. It is sad to think that she was able to communicate with such intensity all that there is to love and to disabuse in the face of this misanthrope... He must have been destroyed or fled, having been put back or he was put down." Surprisingly, in spite of Mary's choice of such an intimate painting genre, she received a number of orders for murals in the United States; in these she employed the same motifs as she had in her canvas paintings. For an exhibition hall in Boston, she painted a pediment with pictures of children, fruit, and flowers.

Breakfast in Bed

1897
Oil on canvas, 65 x 73.6 cm
Virginia Steele Scott Collection,
Huntington Library and Art Gallery,
San Marino, California

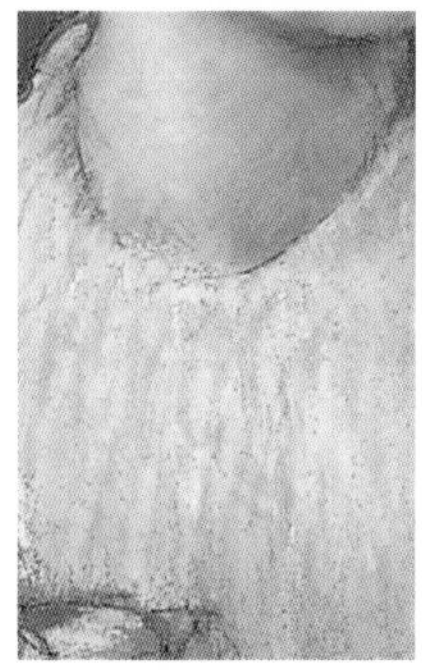

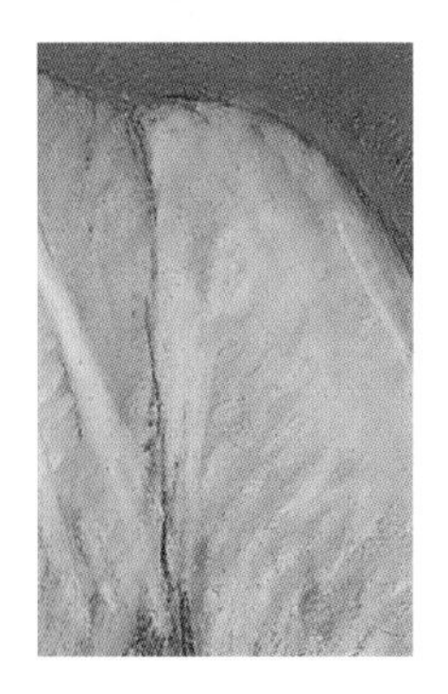

"They said it was a masterpiece, not only because of its conceptualisation and decorative execution, but also because of its style," wrote Ségard. In 1891, the "Woman's Building" was being built for the Chicago World's Columbian Exposition. (It was this very Exposition that is remembered in connection with the tragic death of Carter Harrison, the mayor of Chicago for fourteen years, who was killed three hours before the show's closing, on 28 October 1893). Mary Cassatt and Mary Fairchild MacMonnies, selected from among a dozen applicants, were offered the honour of decorating the large hall of the Woman's Building.

The Cup of Tea

1897
Pastel on tan wove paper, 54.3 x 73 cm
The Estate of Daniel J. Terra, Chicago, Illinois

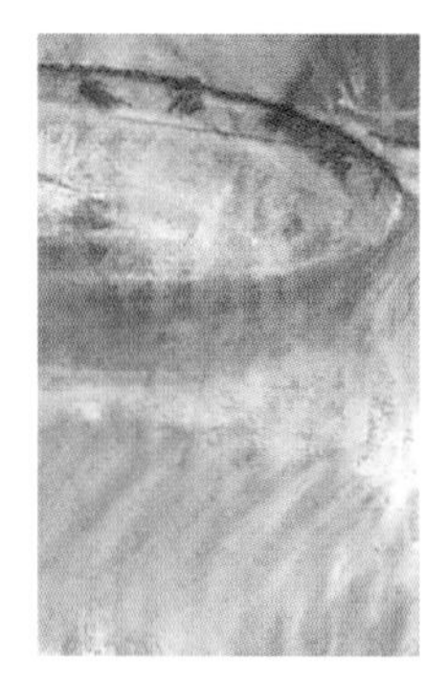

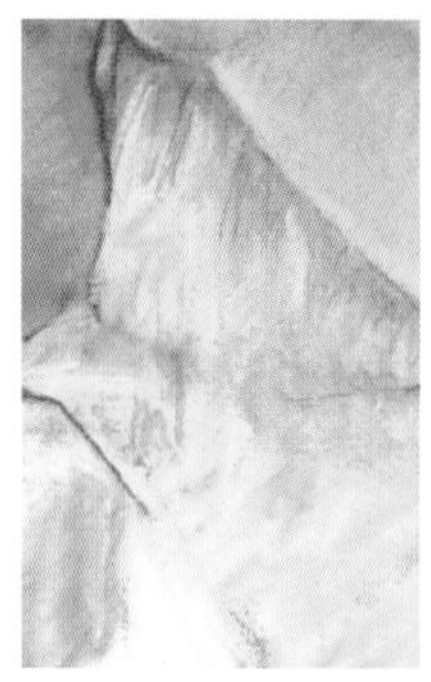

Their task was to decorate two semi-circular tympanums located at two opposite ends of the hall. Like Mary Cassatt, Mary MacMonnies had studied in Paris. Her teacher, Pierre Puvis de Chavannes, was known for a whole series of murals in Paris and other French cities. None of Mary Cassatt's teachers specialised in mural art. Naturally, she wanted to seek the advice of Degas, but did not have the courage. It so happened, however, that Degas knew about Mary's work in Chicago. Camille Pissarro wrote to his son Lucien on 2 October 1892: "Speaking about Miss Cassatt's decoration,

Mother Feeding Her Child

1898
Pastel on wove paper,
mounted on canvas, 64.8 x 81.3 cm
The Metropolitan Museum of Art, New York, NY

mary Cassatt

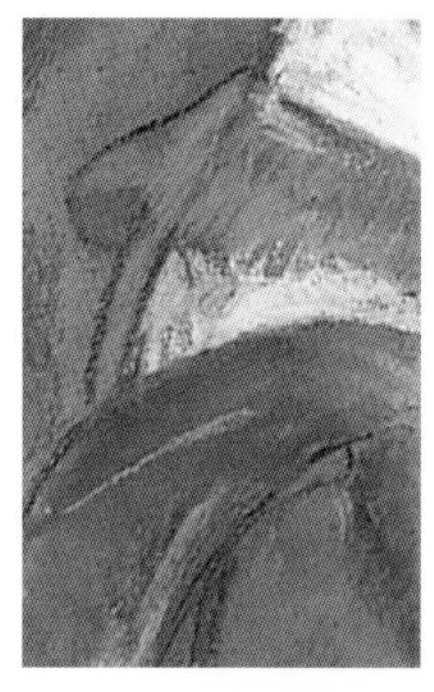

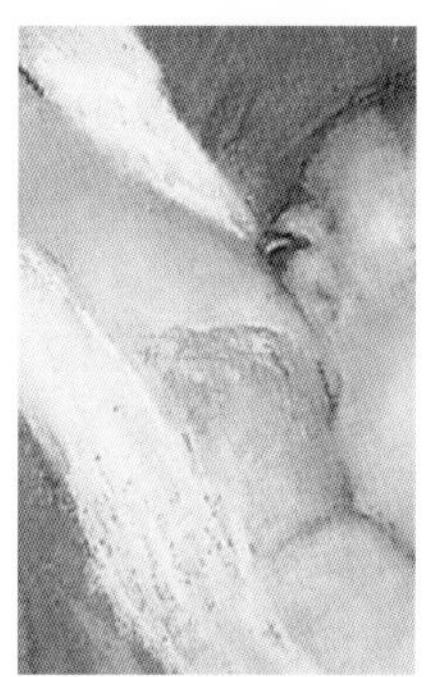

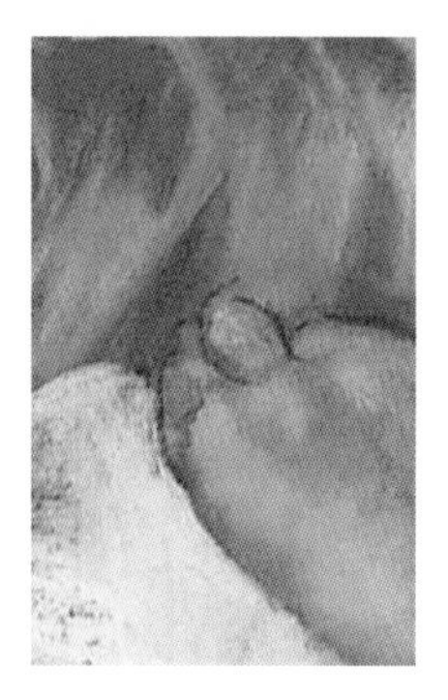

I wish you could have heard the conversation. I had with Degas on what is known as decoration, I am wholly of his opinion; for him it (a decorative mural) is an ornament that should be made with a view to its place in an ensemble, it requires the collaboration of architect and painter. The decorative picture is an absurdity; a picture complete in itself is not a decoration. It seems that even the (decorative paintings of) Puvis de Chavannes don't go well in Lyon, etc., etc."

Young Mother Nursing Her Child

1898
Pastel on tan wove paper, 72.4 x 53.4 cm
Accademia Carrara, Bergamo

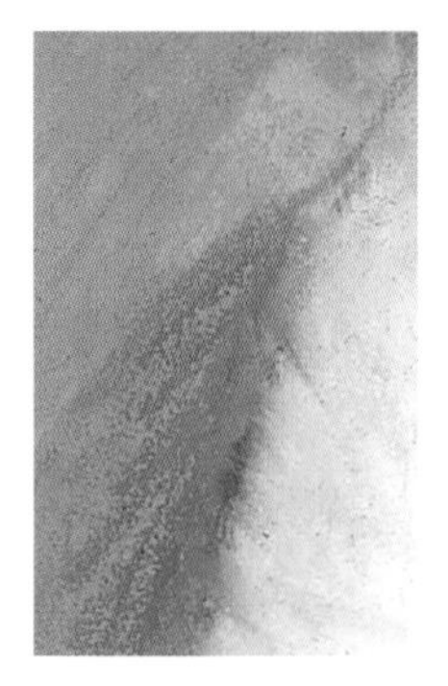

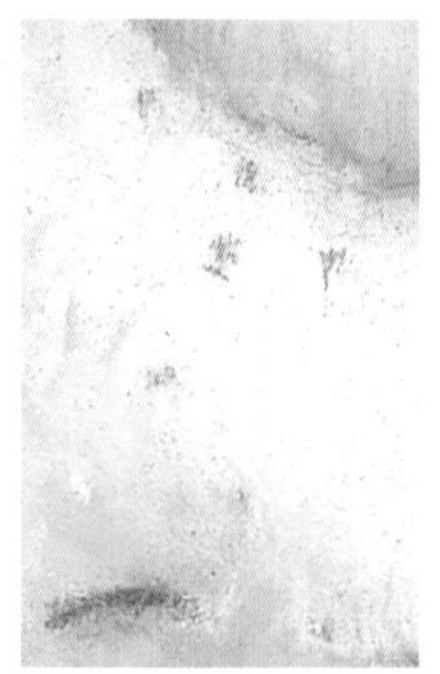

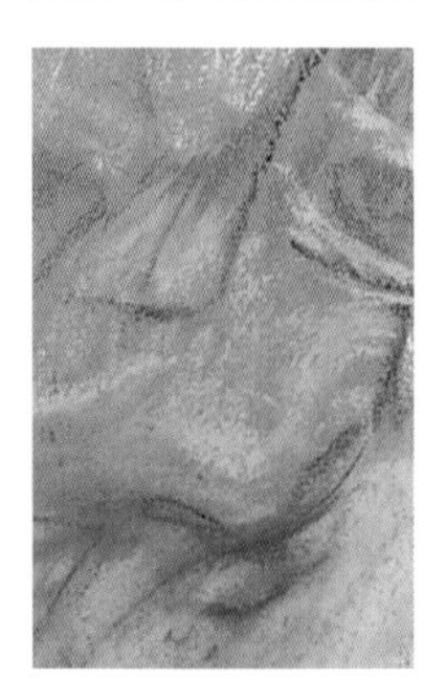

Nevertheless, Mary Cassatt took up this novel task with enthusiasm. According to her own words: "I have enjoyed these new experiences in art immensely." For her tympanum, Mary MacMonnies chose the theme "Primitive Woman", while Mary Cassatt chose "Modern Woman." The artist explained her concept in the following way: "I have tried to express modern woman in the fashions of our day and have tried to represent those fashions as accurately and in as much detail as possible."

Mother and Child

1899
Oil on canvas, 81.6 x 65.7 cm
The Metropolitan Museum of Art, New York, NY

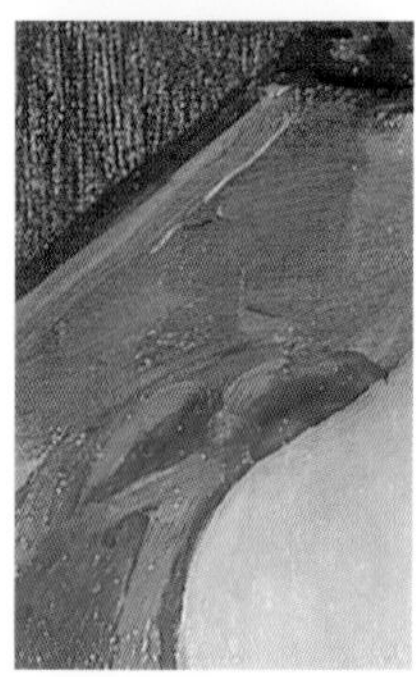

In a letter to one of her customers, she unfolds the symbolism of her art: "I took for the subject of the centre and largest composition young women plucking the fruits of Knowledge and Science. That enabled me to place my figures out-of-doors and allowed of brilliancy of colour. I have tried to make the general effect as bright, as gay, as amusing as possible." When one of Mary's friends asked her whether it was true that she would never paint men, she answered: "I told him it was. Men, I have no doubt, are painted in all their vigour on the walls of the other buildings;

Baby Charles Looking Over
His Mother's Shoulder (No. 3)

1900
Oil on canvas, 71.1 x 50.8 cm
The Brooklyn Museum, New York, NY

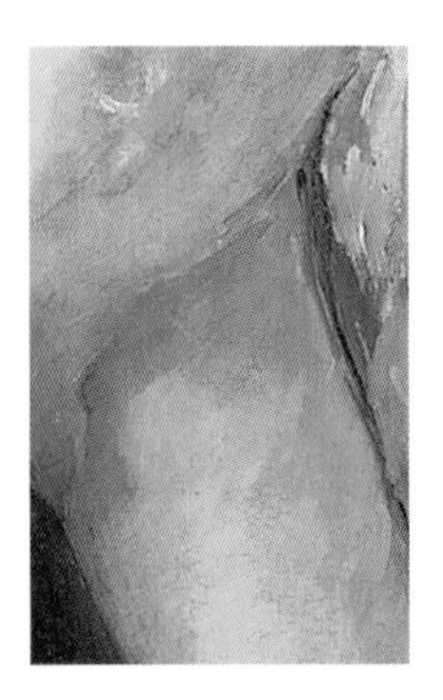

to us the sweetness of childhood, the charm of womanhood (is important); if I have not conveyed some sense of that charm, in one word, if have not been absolutely feminine, then I have failed." Mary herself understood the importance of her role in the feminist movement. Her American contemporaries associated her art with feminism. In those days, it is true, participation in this movement was important in order to gain women's equality with men in the social realm. Time, however, has proved that the work of Mary Cassatt significantly surpasses the

Mother and Child

1900
Pastel on tan wove paper, 71 x 58.5 cm
The Art Institute of Chicago, Illinois

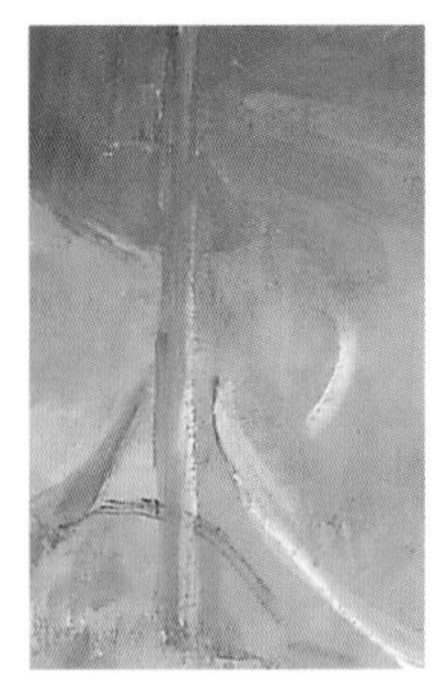

bounds of feminism and deserves its own place in the history of European and American art. In 1905, Mary made a few sketches for the Ladies' Salon in the State Capitol in Harrisburg, the capital of Pennsylvania. She was never actually assigned this project, and all that is preserved is a sketch for the round area above the door showing a group of children next to their mother. None of her murals had the features of decorative art, from the theme and down to the artistic manner. They were not different in any way from paintings on a canvas.

Young Mother

1900
Oil on canvas, 92.4 x 73.7 cm
The Metropolitan Museum of Art, New York, NY

Mary Cassatt

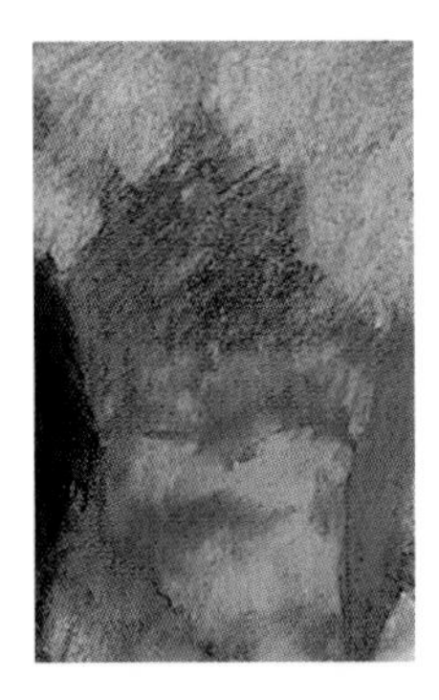

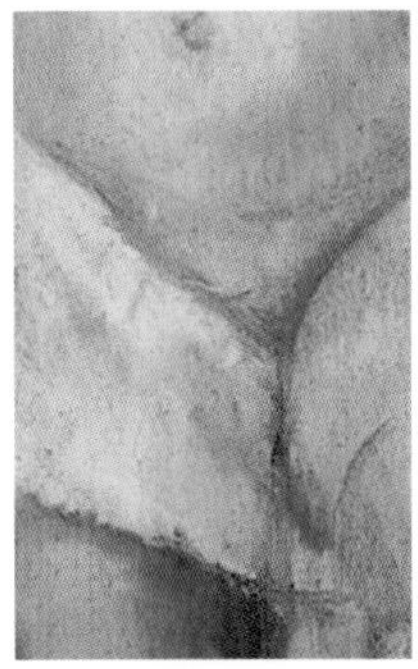

This approach to mural art was characteristic of the Impressionists, as is evident from the words of Degas. Murals painted by Claude Monet and Renoir were not different in terms of composition, colour, or technique from their regular landscapes or city scenes painted *en plein air.* Mary Cassatt's fascination with graphic techniques played a large role in her career. In 1872 in Parma, she met printmaker Carlo Raimondi. It is not clear how interested in etching she was at the time, but she developed her skill wherever possible. Perhaps Mary became interested in etching in her youth, because she loved drawing and strove to perfect it.

## After the Bath

1901
Pastel, 66 x 100 cm
Gift from J. H. Wade,
Cleveland Musuem of Art, Cleveland, Ohio

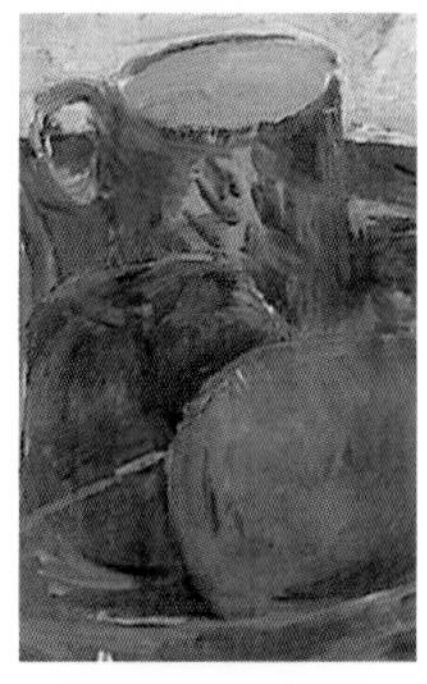

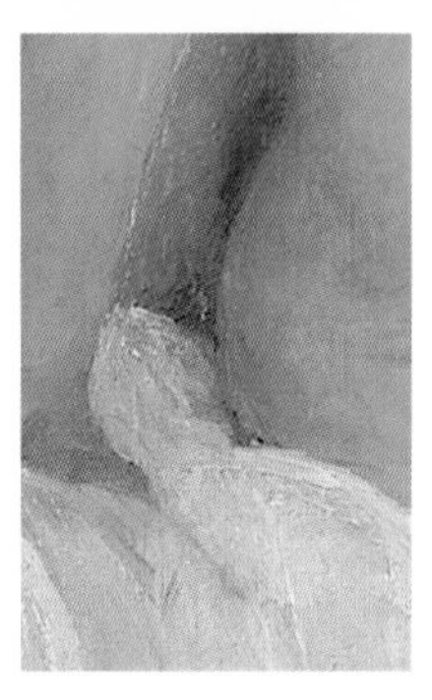

Drawing with a steel graver on a copper plate requires absolute precision and does not allow for mistakes. Mary frequently drew directly onto the plate without preliminary sketches. She once commented in front of one of her prints: "Here is what teaches you how to draw!" She began studying drypoint technique. One of her prints was published on 22nd November 1890 in the *L'Art dans les deux mondes* magazine. Mary mastered aquatint, soft-paint and lithography, and did both black-and-white and colour prints. The subjects of her prints always remained the same women and children as in her paintings, and she sometimes did portraits.

Baby Getting Up from His Nap

1901
Oil on canvas, 92.7 x 73.7 cm
The Metropolitan Musuem of Art, New York, NY

Mary Cassatt

In 1890, together with Degas, Mary visited the Exposition of Japanese Prints, held at the *École des Beaux Arts* in Paris. Impressionists were already familiar with Japanese printmaking and had been studying it. Claude Monet used the Far Eastern perspective of Hok'sai landscapes in his paintings. According to legend, he was the one who stumbled serendipitously upon a stack of Japanese prints in a store in Normandy and brought then to his Impressionist friends. Degas was deeply impressed by the Japanese works at the show, but one can hardly talk about their direct influence on his art – by that time his style was fully formed.

Sara in a Green Bonnet

1901

Oil on canvas, 61 x 91.4 cm

The Smithsonian American Art Museum, Washington D.C.

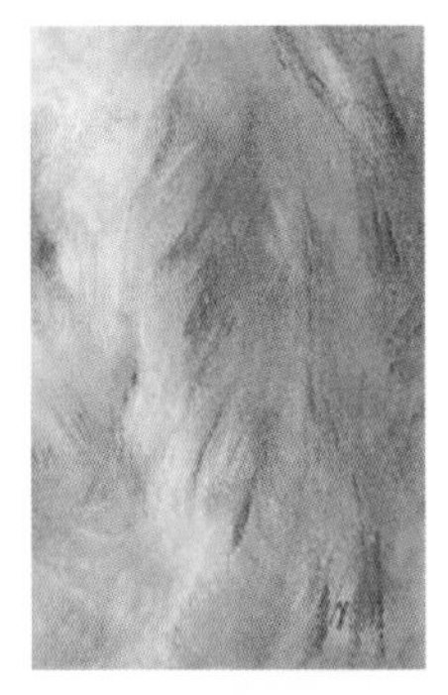

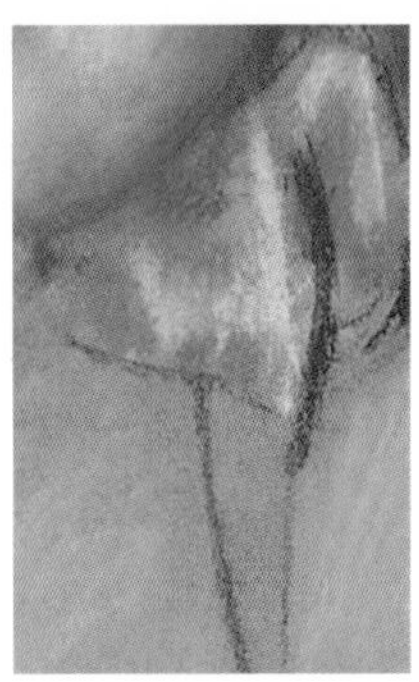

The example of Japanese artists, especially those of Utamaro, master of portraits and the human figure, found immediate and direct reflection in the works of Mary Cassatt, evident already in her paintings made in the 1890s. Perhaps her admiration of Japanese prints influenced her desire to achieve a picture that was clean and crisp, free of superfluous details. Her fascination with the Japanese is reflected in many of her own prints. In the catalogue of an 1891 exhibition, one of her prints was accompanied by the caption:

Woman in a Raspberry Costume

1901
Pastel on paper, 72.7 x 59.6 cm
The Hirshhorn Museum and Sculpture Garden, Washington D.C.

"An attempt to imitate a Japanese print". From the Japanese she learned how to use a flexible line to depict not only movement, but also volume in a human figure. Degas appreciated the mastery she displayed in her colour print *Woman at Her Toilette* (p. 247) (or *Woman Bathing*), "This back, have you modelled it?" he said. Mary Cassatt usually exhibited her prints together with other Parisian printmakers.

Margot Leaning against Her Mother

1902
Drypoint, 24.5 x 17.2 cm
Private Collection

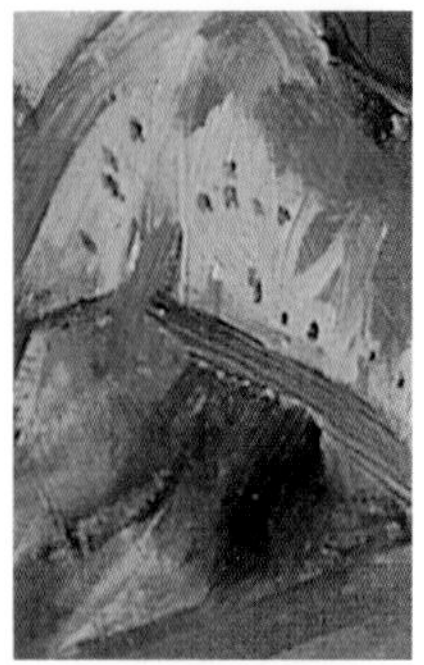

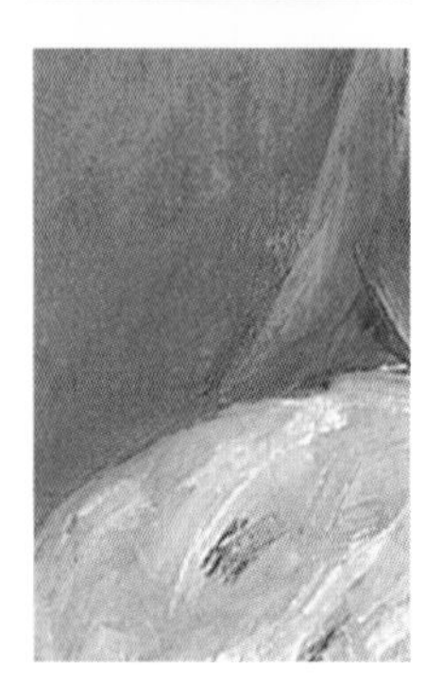

In 1890, they formed the French Society of Artist-Printmakers, headed by Henri Guerard, the husband of Eva Gonzales, the student of Édouard Manet. The term "artist-printmaker" meant a lot in the nineteenth century since for the greater part of the century, printmakers were mere artisans who transferred the paintings of their contemporaries onto black-and-white prints. The word "French", however, excluded Mary from their number. She then asked the Impressionist art dealer Durand-Ruel for a separate hall.

The Caress

1902
Oil on canvas, 94 x 68.6 cm
The Smithsonian American Art Musuem,
Washington D.C.

mary Cassatt

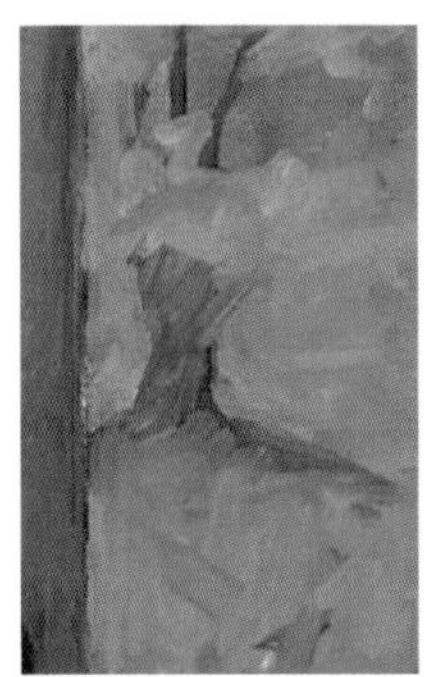

In April 1891, in the gallery of Paul Durand-Ruel, Cassatt's personal show, which included, in addition to her four oil paintings and watercolours, ten of her colour prints, was held. Out of modesty, she indicated in the show's catalogue the name of an artisan printmaker who helped her, which surprised Degas: "Why this man?" he asked. In Degas' opinion, the prints owed their quality to the creator alone. By this time, Mary already had already become a fully mature and original master.

Margot Embracing Her Mother

1902
Oil on canvas, 93 x 73.3 cm
Museum of Fine Arts, Boston, Massachusetts

Mary Cassatt

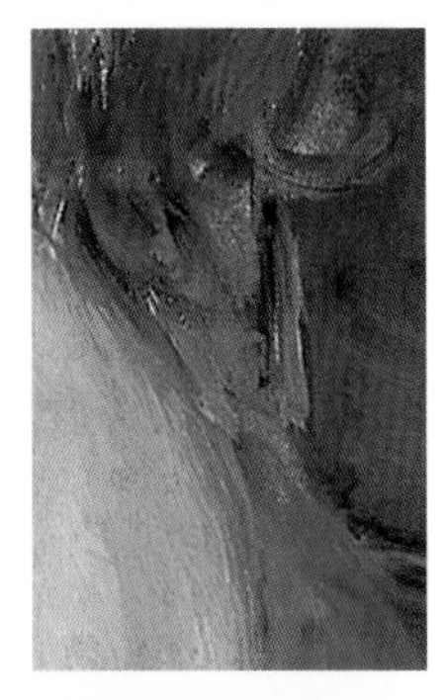

In the show's review, which was published in *Le Chat Noir* on April 11th 1891, Felix Fénéon gave high marks to the paintings and prints by Mary Cassatt. He noted that her works did not have that sentimentality that one would expect from a painter portraying exclusively women and children: "The characters behave normally, and the feeling of permanent maternity gently radiates from the group." Fénéon especially pointed out the quality of the pastels: "The execution of the pastels, a hundred times superior to that of the paintings, is seductive:

Reine Lefebvre Holding a Nude Baby

1902
Oil on canvas, 66 x 55.9 cm
Worcester Art Museum, Worcester, Massachusetts

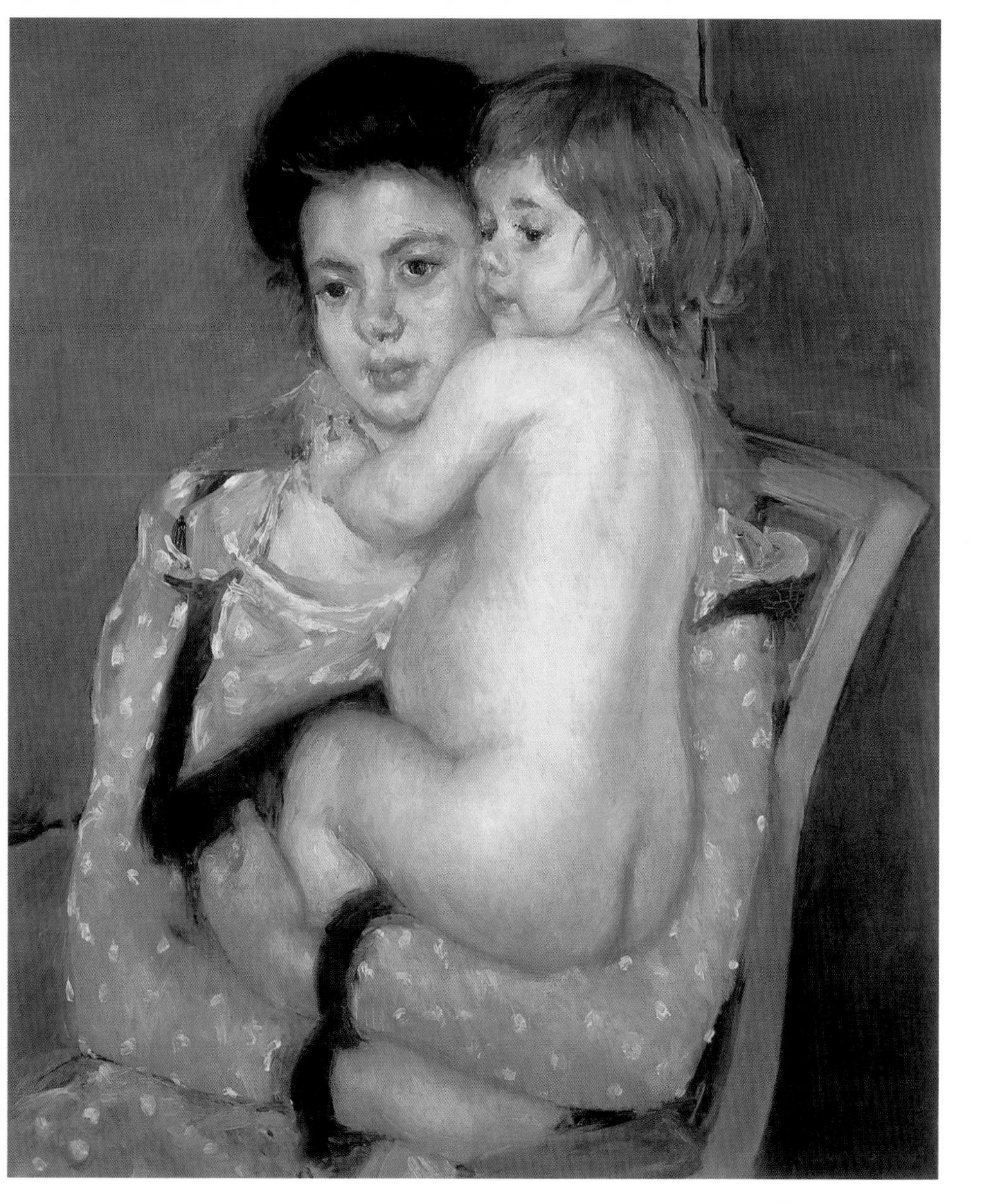

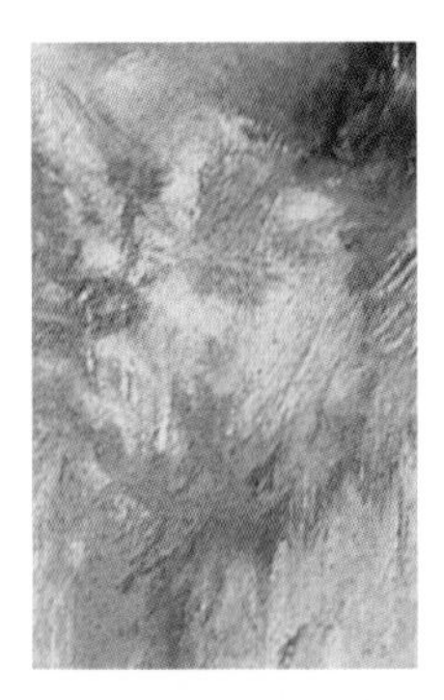

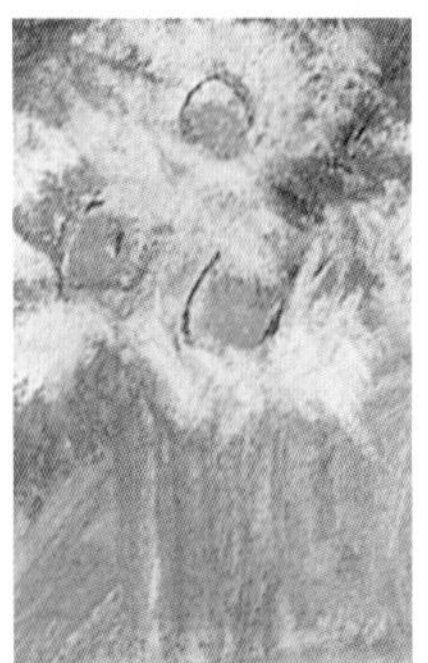

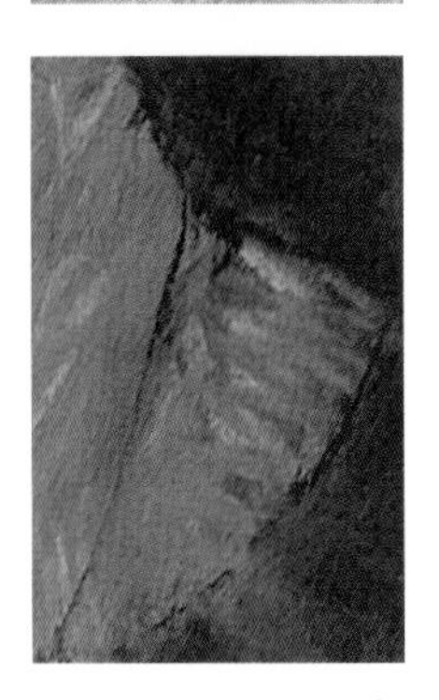

it is supple and active, she depicts at will this nude body of a child, these purple fabrics, plaid, the white of flowers." As to Mary's own confession in the catalogue about her *Imitation de l'Estampe japonaise (Imitation of a Japanese Print)*, Fénéon concluded: "Although she adopts what she wants from the basic conventions of Japanese art, as legitimate as ours, she created in this way the works of intact originality that sum up her sympathy for the masters from over there, instead of allowing them to take her over."

## Margot in Blue

1902
Pastel on paper, 61 x 48.3 cm
The Walters Art Gallery, Baltimore, Maryland

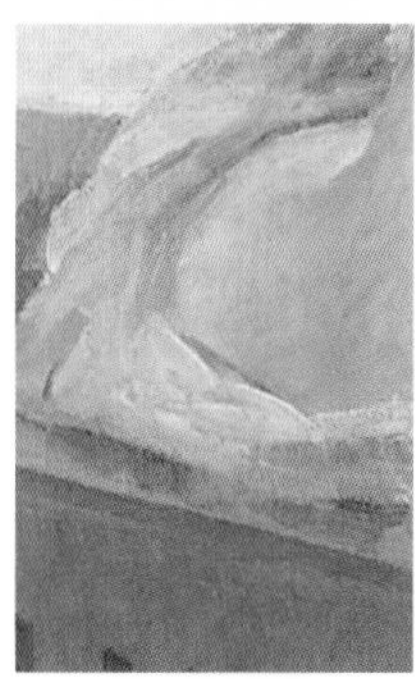

And Fénéon's praise meant a great deal! "Miss Cassatt is an adopted Frenchwoman, but she has remained American," wrote Ségard. Nevertheless, one can hardly say the same about Cassatt's art. Artists did not come to Paris to become French artists. The Parisian School gave them professionalism, let them discover progressive modern art, and helped them find their own individual paths. It is clear that Cassatt realised this completely. However, she did not actually sever her ties with America.

Simone and Her Mother in a Garden

1904
Oil, 24 x 32 cm
The Detroit Institute of Arts, Detroit, Michigan

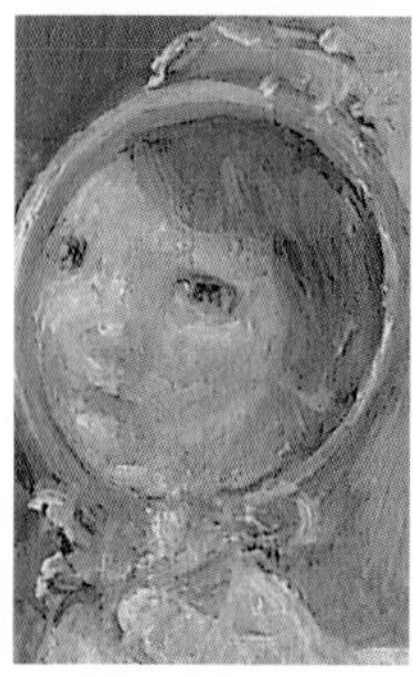

Mary's sister, Lydia, and their mother had already moved to France in 1877, and they travelled throughout Europe. In 1883, Lydia passed away in Paris and, in 1895, Mary's mother died as well. But back in the United States she still had brothers and cousins. And, most importantly, the Pennsylvania Academy of Art constantly exhibited her work. They appear for the first time at a show in Pennsylvania in 1876, even before Mary began exhibiting together with the Impressionists and, starting in 1898, they were shown there every year.

Mother and Child

1905
Oil on canvas, 92.1 x 73.7 cm
The National Gallery of Art, Washington D.C.

mary cassatt

No less important is the fact that, thanks to Mary Cassatt's efforts, American private collections and museums were constantly enriched by European masterpieces. In her youth, in 1873, Mary met an American named Louisine Waldron Elder in Paris, to whom she recommended the purchase of a pastel by Degas, and they remained friends from then onward. When Louisine Waldrone Elder became Mrs H.O. Havemeyer, Mary travelled a great deal with the couple around Europe, finding the best works of old masters for them.

Woman and Child Admiring a Baby

1906
Oil on canvas, 73.7 x 91.4 cm
The Fogg Art Musuem,
Harvard University, Cambridge, Massachusetts

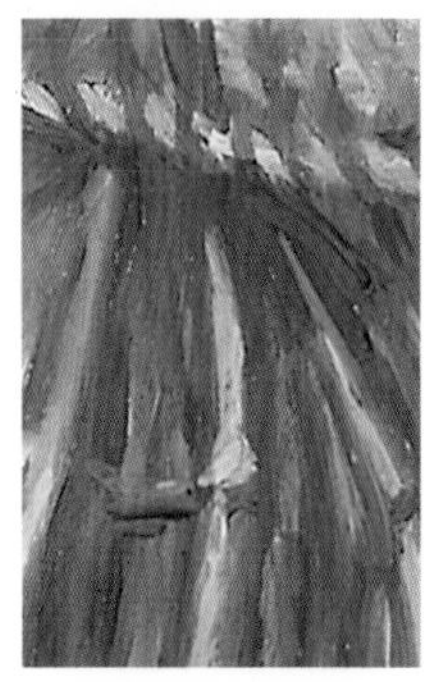

The dealers, Durand-Ruel, played the role of middlemen in these deals, and in her letters to them Mary discussed the purchase by the Havemeyers of paintings by El Greco, Velázquez, Goya, Dürer, Rembrandt, Hals, Manet and the Impressionists. Mary took care that other American collectors brought the best European paintings into the country. "Goya's works go well, wrote to Madame Havemeyer... I will implore her to buy these two beautiful things for the Colonel and to save him from a folly such as acquiring a Hoppner."

Girl in Green

1908
Oil on canvas, 81.3 x 63.5 cm
Gift of Dr Ernest G. Stillman, The City of Art Museum of St Louis, St Louis, Missouri

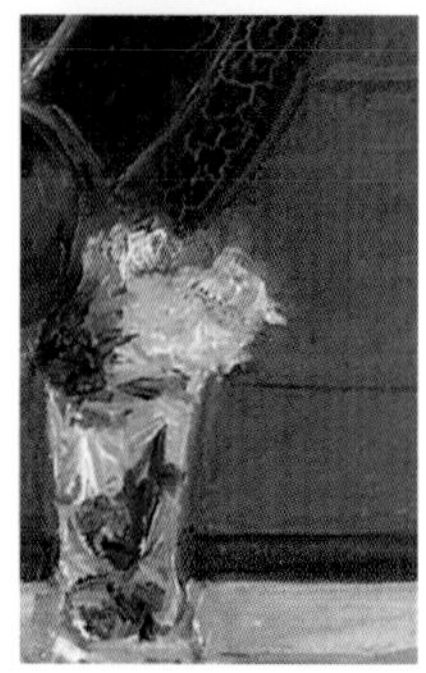

Mary's friends donated many of the paintings they bought to American museums. Mary visited America for the last time in 1908-1909 and refused the distinction of being made an associate member of the National Academy of Design. By this time, she had already been made a member of the *Légion d'Honneur.* In 1914, Mary Cassatt received the Gold Medal of Honor from the Pennsylvania Academy. By this time, she was almost unable to work any more because she was losing her eyesight.

Mother and Child

1908
Oil on canvas, 116.8 x 81.3 cm
The Metropolitan Musuem of Art, New York, NY

The state of her health forced her to spend long months in the South, in Grasse, where she stayed during the whole of World War I. The Mediterranean climate was beneficial for her: "When I arrived, I was not able to walk three hundred metres," she wrote in 1911, "now I do a kilometre and a half without much fatigue." However, for the most part, she resided in the Château de Beaufresne in Mesnil-Théribus (Oise). She bought this castle in 1893 and loved it very much, despite the unpredictable northern climate.

Mother Nursing her Baby

1908
Oil on canvas, 99.1 x 81.3 cm
The Art Institute of Chicago, Illinois

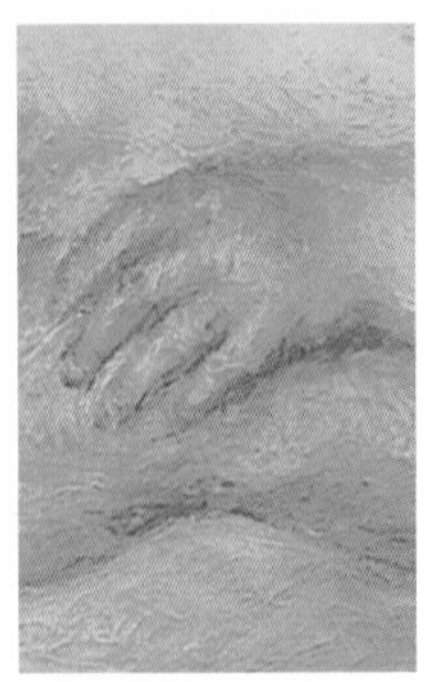

In 1913, in Paris, a monograph by Achille Ségard entitled *A Painter of Children and Mothers: Mary Cassatt* was published and someone immediately offered to translate it into English. His meetings with the artist made a deep impression on Ségard. He describes her as: "Slender and tall, very aristocratic, dressed in black, supporting herself with a cane and moving cautiously through the sandy alleys of her park full of magnificent trees, such was Miss Mary Cassatt as she appeared to me...

Young Mother and Two Children

1908
Oil on canvas, 91.4 x 71.1 cm
The White House, Washington D.C.

Mary Cassatt

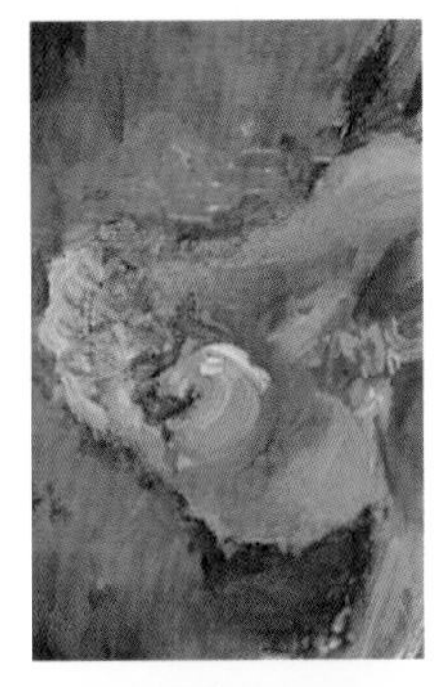

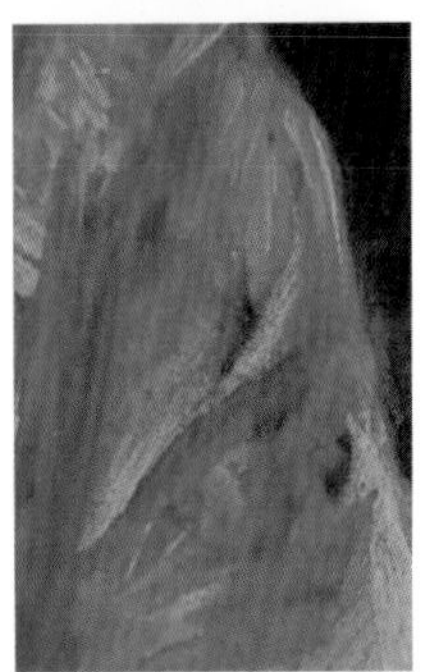

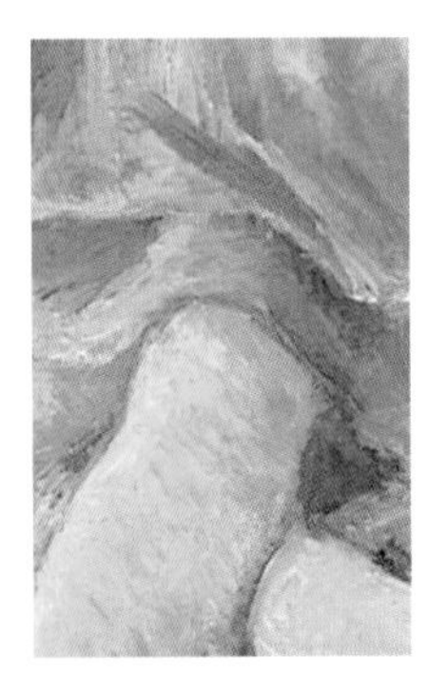

A smile of extreme kindness lit up her serious face, and, along with silver earrings, her grey and blue eyes, of the colour of still water, animated her whole face with its strongly emphasised angles. She offered me an energetic hand that was long, thin, hard-working, and alive, a quivering extension of sensitivity." This enigmatic American died on June 14th 1926, at the age of eighty-two, in her castle in France where she had spent nearly all of her life.

Mother and Child in a Boat

1908
Oil on canvas, 114.3 x 78.7 cm
The Addison Gallery of American Art,
Andover, Massachusetts

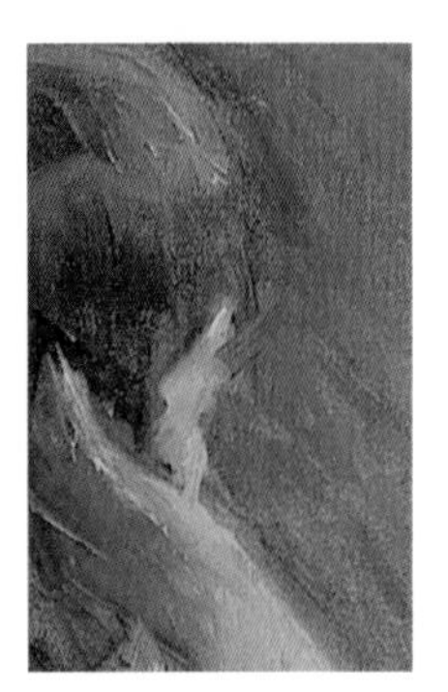

Pissarro, Sisley, and Berthe Morisot had passed away long before, Degas died in 1917, Renoir in 1919. The last of the Impressionists, Claude Monet, died in the same year as Mary Cassatt, in 1926. Mary Cassatt is buried in Château de Beaufresne, where she, too, rests forever in the French earth.

Woman at Her Toilette

1909
Oil on canvas, 92.5 x 72.4 cm
Collection of Mr Fayez Sarofim

# Index